e-pr

e-pr

The Essential Guide to
Public Relations
on the Internet

160201

matt haig

**KOGAN
PAGE**

First published in 2000

Kogan Page Limited
120 Pentonville Road
Londo
N1 9JN
UK

Kogan Page Limited
163 Central Avenue, Suite 2
Dover
NH 03820
USA

British Library Cataloguing in Publication Data

A CIP record for this book is available from the British Library.

ISBN 0 7494 3434 1

Typeset by Saxon Graphics Ltd, Derby
Printed and bound by Creative Print and Design (Wales), Ebbw Vale

contents

Introducing **e-PR**

Although most people in the world of business now accept the significance of the Internet, many still do not understand its terms. This is why so many businesses that sped headlong onto the information superhighway are now left stranded in the lay-by, alone and unvisited in the depths of cyberspace. The fact is that too many businesses are too busy thinking about what they want from the Internet, to consider the demands of their online market.

The Internet was not originally intended for commercial use. Instead, it was designed as a communication tool that aided the distribution of information. Those businesses that are succeeding online today, do so by recognizing the Internet's original purpose. Although their ultimate aim may be to sell more of Product X or Service Y, they understand that to achieve this they must communicate valuable information and engage in mutually beneficial relations with their audience.

The key to business success online is therefore to have a PR (or public relations) perspective: to build and manage reputation by communicating information and listening to the demands of an online public. Of course, good communication has always been important in the business world; it's just that with the arrival of the Internet age it has become essential.

While businesses must change their notion of how the Internet can work for them by thinking in terms of PR, they must also change their notion of PR itself. Public relations on the Internet has a much bigger and broader role to play than they do in the so-called 'real world'. As every aspect of a company's online activity has the power to affect its public relations, information and communication must be managed with much greater care.

This new medium therefore brings with it a new form of marketing, in which the online point of contact between a firm and its public is everything. To give a name to this new Internet marketing, we shall call it **e-PR**.

About this book

On the subject of communication, this book is intended to communicate valuable and relevant information to the following audiences:

- business owners and managers;
- marketing managers;
- PR professionals;
- business, marketing and PR students;
- Web site managers;
- anyone else interested in e-business, marketing or PR.

If you fit into any of the above categories, e-PR (the book and the discipline) is relevant to you and could dramatically change your view of e-business and the Internet in general.

This book will not try to convince you of the importance of the Internet to the business world. The fact that you decided to pick up this book means you probably understand this already. Instead, what this book aims to do is to explore and explain the principles and practice of e-PR. This will help to provide you with the focus you need to make your Internet marketing a success.

Even if you ignore PR in the real world, on the Internet it is unavoidable. Everything you do online can and should be seen as an e-PR activity. This book therefore gives you everything you need to build successful long-term relationships with the people who matter to your e-business, enabling you to put the power of e-PR into practice.

Amongst other things, this book will help you to:

- think from an e-PR perspective;
- conduct market research on the Internet;
- develop market research on the Internet;
- develop a Web site, which will build and maintain business relations;
- get a good position on the major search engines;
- use e-mails more effectively;
- send out online newsletters;
- monitor and contribute to online discussion groups;
- conduct press relations online;
- integrate your e-PR activity with real world PR.

What is e-PR?

e-PR refers to public relations on the Internet. But what exactly does that mean? Let's spell it out:

- **e is for electronic.** As the online revolution takes off, so does the popularity of the fifth letter of the alphabet. The 'e' in e-PR is the same 'e' that comes before mail and commerce to refer to the electronic medium of the Internet. E-PR concerns every aspect of the Internet, including e-mail systems as well as the World Wide Web.
- **P is for public.** The idea of a singular public is now an outdated one. It is more useful to think in terms of different publics or audiences. This is particularly the case with the Internet that accommodates a near infinite variety of niche markets and micro-communities.
- **R is for relations.** Building relations between your business and its audiences is the key to success on the Internet. Thousands of one-to-one relations can be built up simultaneously on the Internet due to its interactive nature. The Internet is therefore the most powerful relation-building tool the business world has ever witnessed.

The e-PR difference

The most significant difference between online and offline PR is that in the real world PR depends on an intermediary or gatekeeper, typically a journalist. When you want to communicate with your audience via the traditional media, you have two unsatisfactory choices:

1. Send press releases or other material to a journalist, hoping he or she will take an interest in what you have to say.
2. Spend money on advertising space.

On the Internet, you can bypass both of these options and communicate directly with your audience via your Web site, e-mail messages and discussion group contributions. In addition to this, the Internet lends e-PR other considerable advantages:

- **Constant communication.** The Internet is an insomniac. It enables you to communicate with people 24 hours a day, 7 days a week, 365 days a year.
- **Instant response.** You can respond instantly to emerging issues and market developments via the Internet.
- **Global audience.** Geographical limitations are all but eliminated when you are online. You can communicate with clients in Singapore, investors in Saudi Arabia and journalists in San Francisco at no extra expense.
- **Audience knowledge.** Because the Internet is interactive, you can get constant feedback from your audience. This takes out the guesswork by helping you understand what your audience wants.
- **Two-way communication.** Two-way communication between an organization and its publics is a major PR goal, as it helps build strong and mutually beneficial relationships. In the real world it is rarely possible as the traditional media confine the involvement of the audience to that of a passive spectator. On the Internet, two-way communication is made possible by allowing the audience to interact with you and your business.
- **Cost-effective.** While PR in the real world is considered more cost-effective than advertising, e-PR is even more cost-effective as there are no stationery or printing costs involved. Furthermore, as Internet rates get even cheaper, e-PR's cost-effectiveness increases.

E is for everything

The 'e' in e-PR may stand for 'electronic' but it could also stand for 'everything'. This is because everything you do online should be considered a PR activity. In the real world you can choose to keep things from the media, but online you are automatically a part of the media and operate from within them.

Whereas in the real world you can keep prying eyes away from your office, your Web site can be viewed by anyone. Competitors, investors, journalists and hostile customers can all visit your site or read the messages and articles you post to online newsgroups. On the Internet, you are permanently exposed to the outside world, and so everything you put online can affect your reputation.

More than Web sites

Your Web site is in many ways the online face of your company, and is probably the most important thing to get right when attempting to build relations online. Although your Web site needs to be at the centre of your e-PR activity, there are many other ways you can build relations on the Internet.

E-mail is the most widely used part of the Internet and can be a very useful e-PR tool. E-mail is being used increasingly by business managers to communicate quickly with employees and colleagues. Furthermore, you can send online newsletters via e-mail to different target audiences. E-mail is being used more and more as a way of 'getting the word out' about a product or service. In the United States, for instance, Ford Motor Company recently used a comprehensive e-mail campaign. They sent out brochures, newsletters and flyers via e-mail and set up a chat room to hold an online conference.

E-mail and Web-based discussion groups are also a big e-PR concern. It is important to monitor these online groups in order to prevent misinformation spreading about your business, and to keep an eye on what people are saying about you and your competition.

Have an e-PR perspective

E-PR is not a part of Internet marketing; it is a type of Internet marketing. That is to say that it provides a way of viewing the whole online marketing process, from promoting your site through to the way you sell your products and services. The Internet is about interactivity and information, which provide the foundation for all e-PR activity.

Thinking from an e-PR perspective will therefore help you maximize the chances of e-business success, by taking the Internet on its own terms. Having an e-PR perspective involves learning the new three Rs:

   Relations. E-PR is about building relations through interacting with your different audiences. Successful relations are long-term and mutually beneficial.

- **Reputation.** Reputation is your most important business asset. E-PR is the art of managing your online reputation. Boosting, preserving and consolidating it are essential for long-term success.
- **Relevance.** You need to make sure that everything you put online is directly relevant to your audience. There are many Web sites that appear irrelevant but in fact aren't. Absolut Vodka (www.absolut.com), for instance, has a Web site all about DJs and clubbing which hardly mentions vodka at all. It works because it is very relevant to the interests of the image-conscious youth market whom Absolut targets.

By making all your online activity conform to one or all of these three Rs, you will be taking on board an e-PR perspective.

Narrowcasting

The Internet's interactivity enables people to customize information to their own specific needs. One hundred Internet users could visit the same Web site and come away with completely different information. The paradox of the Internet, therefore, is that it allows you to communicate with a lot of people on a one-to-one level. Whereas traditional media **broad**casts the same message to a mass audience, the Internet **narrow**casts messages to individual groups within the same audience. You can therefore build up thousands of one-to-one relationships simultaneously. In a world of niche markets and ever-smaller population segments, the Internet therefore has the potential to become the perfect communication tool enabling you to target 'audiences of one'.

E-PR versus advertising

The Internet is being increasingly seen as a medium more suited to public relations than advertising. In fact, many successful Internet-based companies, such as the popular search engine AltaVista, spend nothing at all on advertising. Of those companies that do consider advertising to be important, such as AOL, Yahoo! and

Lycos, far more money is spent advertising on traditional media such as TV than on advertising online. Furthermore, companies that sacrifice PR activity for expensive online and offline advertising campaigns end up being publicly criticized for failing to deliver. This proved to be the case for the ill-fated and much maligned online urban-sportswear store, Boo.com. After neglecting PR to concentrate on a high-profile international advertising campaign, it soon found itself the focus of negative publicity. Realizing too late that it needed to cut back on advertising to concentrate on PR, Boo.com ceased trading in April 2000 (see Figure 1.1).

So, why is the Internet not the advertiser's paradise it was once heralded to be? There are three main reasons:

- The Internet is a 'pull-me' medium. This means Internet users pull information towards them and therefore have complete control over what they choose to take a look at; generally, people do not choose to look at advertising.

Figure 1.1 Boo.com's PR campaign

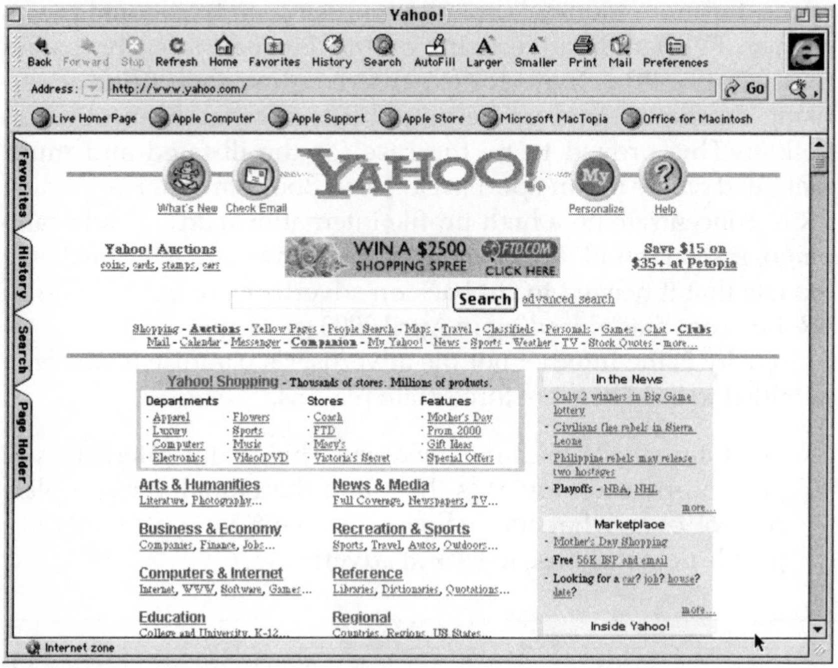

Figure 1.2 The world's largest search engine Yahoo! is popular with online advertisers

- People want information. They go online to find solutions to problems, and want to make educated decisions based on logic and reason. In this context, the hard sell only serves to irritate not stimulate.
- The Internet lets you control messages. Advertising works in the 'real world' because it gives companies the opportunity to say what they want, without having to rely on journalists. The Internet gives you that control automatically, without making you pay for it.

In addition, online advertising has the following drawbacks:

- The CPM system. Payment for online advertising is usually based on CPM or cost per thousand page impressions (the M refers to the Roman numeral for a thousand). That means the cost for the ad to be loaded onto a specific Web site 1,000 times. This does not guarantee your ad will be seen, however, as often ads are placed at the bottom of the page, out of view to the visitor unless he or she decides to scroll down. CPM rates vary widely (from 500 US cents to US $500).

- Banner swaps don't work. Many businesses, put off by online advertising rates, are attracted by the prospect of 'free advertising' available at banner exchange sites. However, you will have a very limited choice as to where, when and how your ad appears on other sites. Furthermore, the swap is never an equal one. For every two times you display another ad, your ad will appear somewhere else only once.
- Click through rates are very low. Click through refers to someone clicking on an ad to visit a Web site. Yahoo! claims that its advertisers receive a click through rate of only two per cent (see Figure 1.2).

Other online advertising methods such as newsletter and e-mail ads have an even lower success rate than Web-based banner advertising.

There are times when Internet advertising can be effective. If you are big enough and willing to take a risk, online advertising could be worth it. Amazon, for instance, spends millions on Internet ads to build its brand online. While they admit this does not lead to instant profits, they maintain it creates customer loyalty, which will be valuable in the long term. If you can afford to take such expensive risks, advertising may be a valid option but only if you integrate it, as Amazon do, with effective e-PR activity. If you do want to give online advertising a go, you should check out Ad-Guide (http://www.ad-guide.com/), the most comprehensive resource for e-advertising.

Summary

E-PR is not just a series of techniques; it provides a whole new perspective to Internet marketing. To survive and succeed online, businesses need to **relate** to, as well as sell to, their audiences.

Companies that try to import traditional corporate marketing solutions into cyberspace will have to struggle in order to survive. The traditional one-way hard sell mentality must therefore be resisted in favour of an approach more in tune with the interactive capabilities of the Internet. This approach needs to be based on understanding your audience and helping your audience understand you. Reputation, relevance and relations are the keywords attached to this e-PR approach. The rest of this book will be devoted to helping you make the Internet work for you by putting e-PR into practice.

two

E-PR **preparation**

Before you embark on an e-PR campaign, you need to consider what you want to achieve and how you want to achieve it. This chapter will look at what you should think about when deciding your e-PR objectives and strategy. We will also discuss the importance of targeting your online audiences.

Your e-PR objectives

The first thing you need to decide is what exactly you want to achieve from e-PR. Research (which is discussed in the next chapter) can help formulate your objectives, but even before you think about research you need to have some idea of your goals. Writing down objectives at the start gives you a yardstick by which you can measure your success, as well as a clear direction in which to head.

Before deciding your specific e-PR objectives, you need to think broadly about what you think the Internet can help you achieve. Here are some possibilities:

- to expand your business;
- to sell more of your product or service online;
- to sell more of your product or service offline;
- to win support;
- to launch your business, product or service;
- to win over public opinion;
- to make more money.

Once you have done this, you need to think from the perspective of your audience. They are not interested in how much money you make, or in helping to boost your online profile. They just want to satisfy their own objectives. If you can see things from their perspective, you are more likely to come up with an objective that will direct your online activity in the right direction.

Essentially your e-PR objectives should contain two elements: what you want a business to achieve (for you and your audience), and the times you want to achieve it by. When putting these two elements together you need to:

- **Be specific.** Vague objectives, such as 'To get as many visitors to my site', 'To generate maximum online publicity' or 'To meet the demands of my online audience' are unhelpful. Your objective should be clear and provide focus. For instance, Federal Express stated that their e-PR objective was to provide up-to-date unfiltered news on their Web site.
- **Be realistic.** Don't expect too much, too soon. 'To establish Better Books as a leading online specialist in crime fiction over the next twelve months' is a more realistic objective than 'To be better known than Amazon in six months' time'.
- **Think of your audience.** By thinking in terms of how you can help your audience, you will be approaching e-PR from the right angle. It may even be a good idea to come up with different objectives relating to different audiences: customers, investors, employees, competitors, the media, industry figures and so on. However, if you do this, make sure the objectives complement, not contradict one another. When you have decided upon an objective, send it via e-mail to your colleagues and employees in capital letters. Singing from the same hymn sheets is perhaps the most important e-PR lesson of all.

Your e-PR strategy

Your e-PR objective represents where you want to be; your e-PR strategy consists of how you are going to get there. While your e-PR objective may only concern your Web site, the online strategy you use to promote your site will inevitably cover areas beyond your site such as e-mail and discussion groups. You need a strategy to keep you on track. Your individual tactics may change but your strategy should remain fundamentally the same. To implement a successful strategy you will need to:

- Have a purpose (your objective should provide you with this).
- Conduct research to discover which online methods will be right for your business and its audience.
- Put a plan together based on your objectives and your research.
- Make sure you have all the resources, human and otherwise, needed to carry out the plan.

Targeting audiences

On the Internet, people are provided with more choice than any other medium and are able to personalize information to a much greater extent. To be able to build successful relations online you need to understand exactly whom you are targeting. Your online communication needs to **relate** to people as well as convey information.

Although PR stands for **public** relations, there are in fact several different audiences that may affect your business online (as opposed to one general public). These audiences may include:

- customers;
- potential customers;
- other consumers;
- investors;
- competitors;
- trade organizations;
- journalists;
- industry figures;
- search engine review staff;
- discussion group moderators;
- employees;
- online regulators;
- online sponsors;
- online advertisers;
- pressure groups;
- companies with links to and from your site.

Within each individual audience, there are further distinctions you will need to make. For instance, you should try to distinguish between the types of customer you plan to target. You can do this by looking at the following factors:

- **Age.** You may produce a spot cover-up that targets the youth market, as well as a grey hair cover-up aimed at a more mature market.
- **Geography.** Although the Internet is a global phenomenon, cultural differences remain and should be acknowledged.
- **Gender.** Different product lines may appeal to different sexes.
- **Socio-demographics.** You may want to target markets that fall into different socio-demographic groupings.
- **Internet usage.** You can distinguish between heavy and occasional Internet users.
- **Loyalty.** Your audience may be divided between loyal and impulsive or opportunistic customers.

These are quantifiable distinctions that can be made, but there may also be more subtle differences between customers relating to lifestyle choices and attitudes. This may all appear daunting but it demonstrates the need to view the Internet as being comprised of a near infinite amount of niche audiences.

You should break down your audiences into as many categories, sub-categories and even sub-sub-categories as you can in order to build and sustain mutually beneficial relations. After you have done this, you should *prioritize* which audiences are most important to you and your business. This will help you decide what to include on your site and other e-material. For instance, if you decide to target investors, you could publish your financial reports online. However, you do not have to limit your e-PR efforts to one target audience. The Internet's interactive nature means that, via e-mail or on the Web, you can customize information for separate audiences in a number of ways:

- Provide different language options. If you are targeting an international audience, you could provide different language options for your Web site and other online material.
- Have several Web sites. Global brands such as Durex and Guinness have sites for separate countries or products linked by one home page (see Figure 2.1).
- Divide your Web site into categories relating to the requirements of individual audiences.
- Have different e-mail addresses and e-mail boxes for each product and service.
- Get links from a cross-section of sites appealing to different types of people.

Figure 2.1 Durex is a global brand that acknowledges geographical differences on its Web site

▨ Contribute to newsgroups covering topics relevant to specific audiences.

Getting the right information

The way relations between you and your audience are built up online is via information: they want it, you provide it. Once you have worked out which audiences you are going to target, you need to think about the information you want them to receive. To make sure your online information is relevant to your audiences you also need to think about the message your audiences want to receive. Remember that Internet users 'pull' information towards them and you can only push it so far in their direction. Your audience only volunteers to take part in any sort of online relationship with your business based on the quality of information you provide. The information that you put on your site and in online material needs to be:

- **Clear.** Information in Web sites, newsletters, e-mails and so on needs to be easy to understand and serve a definite and identified purpose.
- **Exclusive.** Your online information should ideally be exclusive so your audience cannot access it elsewhere on the Internet.
- **Relevant.** The information you provide needs to be relevant to the requirements of your target audience. Internet users go online to find solutions to problems and answers to questions. What relevant solutions can you provide?
- **Accurate.** Relationships are built on trust. You therefore need to assure your audience that all the information you give them is accurate by supporting claims with facts.

Summary

The fact that the Internet is a medium that **narrowcasts** messages to diverse audiences means that you need to direct your e-PR efforts carefully. To conduct effective e-PR you must clarify your objectives, construct a strategy and identify your audience. In order to do this successfully you will also need to conduct research, the topic of our next chapter.

three

E-PR and research

Research should provide the foundation of any effective e-PR campaign. It helps you to direct your e-PR efforts by helping you to identify key audiences, locate target media and plan the right strategy. This chapter discusses the way research should be integrated into your e-PR activity, and how it should be conducted effectively.

The importance of Internet research

Worldwide there are estimated to be over 300 million people using the Internet on a regular basis, and this number is increasing daily. The number of Web pages out there is even greater. The Internet is therefore a very big place, and without researching the users or sites your e-PR should target, your e-business will remain lost in the realms of cyberspace. In PR terms, research is even more essential online than it is in the real world due to the sheer size and diversity of the Internet.

There are seven main aims of research in relation to e-PR:

- to help you determine your e-PR objectives and strategies;
- to monitor and track e-PR activities already under way;
- to evaluate the outcome, impact or effectiveness of an e-PR campaign;
- to help predict and prevent online issues developing into crises;
- to help promote your e-business by providing useful publicity material;
- to keep track of competitors;
- to determine media you should target in e-media campaigns.

To help you understand, however, why research is so integral to e-PR, we should look at the uses it can serve.

The ultimate research tool

While the Internet renders research essential, it also makes it a whole lot easier. The Internet contains not only a near infinite amount of information, but it also provides you with tools which make locating the information you want a relatively simple process. Moreover, it enables you to conduct both primary research (by allowing you to communicate with your audiences directly) and secondary research (by trawling through the information brought up by search engines).

Search engines as research tools

The most obvious way to conduct research on the Internet is via the major search engines and online directories such as:
Yahoo! (http://www. yahoo.com), AltaVista (http://www. altavista. com) and Lycos (http:// www.lycos.com).

A search engine is a database that retrieves information, based on words or a phrase that you enter. When you carry out a search, the engine looks through its database to find entries that match the information you entered. This means you can conduct keyword searches that will help you to find the audiences relevant to your business, as well as enable you to keep track of your competitors' e-PR strategies. AltaVista and Yahoo! are particularly useful research tools as they allow you to fine-tune your searches in a number of ways.

To find the sites you need, you should know how to use the search engines to your best advantage. Here are some tips on using search engines effectively:

- Use more than one engine. Search engines categorize different sites in different ways, so use several of them.
- Be as specific as possible. Typing in 'chocolate éclair' will result in a more specific search than if you used the keyword 'cakes'.
- Conduct Boolean searches. A Boolean search is where you use 'Boolean operators' such as '+', 'OR' and 'NOT' in keyword

searches. To make your searches more specific you can place one of these tags between keywords to provide the engine with more direction. For instance, you could type in:

- 'Richard Branson + Virgin' to find pages relating to both Richard Branson and Virgin; or
- 'Richard Branson OR Virgin' to find pages relating either to Richard Branson or Virgin; or
- 'Richard Branson NOT Virgin' to find pages related to Richard Branson, but only if these pages do not mention Virgin.

The word 'Boolean' refers to George Boole, a 19th-century English mathematician who produced a selection theory on which Boolean searches are founded.

Narrowing a search using AltaVista

AltaVista is a great search engine for e-PR purposes because it offers users certain keywords to fine-tune their searches (see Figure 3.1). Here are some of the more useful ones:

- Adding '+domain.com' to your keywords limits a search to dot com sites. This keyword can also help you conduct nation-specific searches. For instance, you could add '+ domain.co.uk' for a search of all UK sites or '+domain: co.uk' for a search of UK sites or '+domain: fr' for a French search.
- Adding a Web site address after 'link:' will help you find Web pages that link to that address.
- Placing 'text:' at the start of your keyword search will help you limit a search to text only. Image files and links will therefore be ignored.
- Using 'title:' before your keyword(s) is a particularly effective way of narrowing down your search, as it only brings up Web pages that have the keyword in the title rather than the text itself.
- The prefix 'url:' will help you narrow a search even further by only searching for keywords in Web site addresses (URLs).

Narrowing a search using Yahoo!

With over 40 million visitors a month, Yahoo! is the most popular search site of all. Like AltaVista, Yahoo! helps you to narrow a

Figure 3.1 AltaVista enables you to narrow your search engine in a variety of ways

search beyond your own keywords, by creating different sections that you can select. By clicking on the Options button at Yahoo!'s home page, you will be provided with a form that will help you limit your search.

You can narrow searches to specific topics (such as 'computers') or geographical areas (such as 'UK and Ireland' or 'London').

For a comprehensive comparison of search engines, visit the Search Engine Watch site (http://www.searchenginewatch.com).

Searching the search engines

There are a number of so-called 'meta-search sites' which allow you to search several different engines simultaneously. Here are three of the main ones:

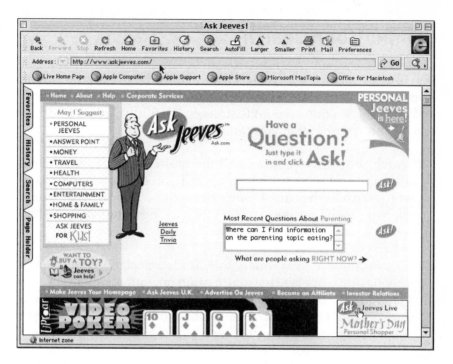

Figure 3.2 Ask Jeeves enables you to conduct searches in plain English

- Ask Jeeves (http://www.askjeeves.com). Ask Jeeves allows you to ask questions and commands in plain English such as 'Find me everything on Internet PR' or 'Where is Timbuktu?' (see Figure 3.2).
- Mamma (http://www.mamma.com). The Mamma search engine searches AltaVista, Yahoo!, Excite, Infoseek, Lycos, WebCrawler and HotBot. It also allows you to limit searches down to page titles.
- MetaCrawler (http://www.metacrawler.com). MetaCrawler also allows you to narrow your search. Click the Power Search button and make your selections on the search form.

How to register with the search engines is discussed in detail in Chapter 7 of this book.

Competitor research

One of your main research objectives should be to keep an eye on your competitors' e-PR efforts. Information on your competitors will help guide your own e-PR strategy. To find relevant information on your competition you can:

- Search the search engines. All the main search sites can find company and industry information if you use appropriate keywords such as the competitor's name (if you know it) or words referring to the business sector (such as 'pest control' or 'estate agents').
- Search competitors' sites.
- Look for trade associations online. Trade associations are usually a good source of objective information on your competition.
- Search discussion groups. Discussion groups (which are discussed in more detail later on in this book) are online bulletin boards for people interested in certain topics. Some groups are likely to discuss your competition.
- Read mailing lists. Mailing lists serve a similar function to discussion groups except that the messages are sent directly to your e-mail address. (You can find a comprehensive list of mailing lists at http://www.neosoft.com/Internet/paml.)
- If you are researching public limited companies, visit Daily Stocks (http://www.dailystocks.com) which links to a variety of sites providing information on companies on international stock markets.
- Monitor online trade publications. Virtually all print-trade publications have an online presence. Often their online version has more up-to-date information and an archive of previous issues.

Researching discussion groups

One of your research objectives should be to find out not only what people are saying about themselves on the Web, but also what they are saying to one another in the Internet's thousands of newsgroups and mailing list discussion groups. Researching these groups will serve to help you:

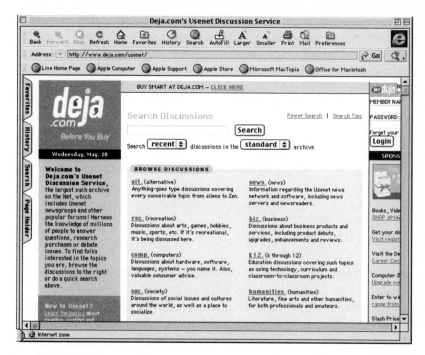

Figure 3.3 DejaNews provides access to around 100,000 discussion groups that you can search by keyword or phrase

- Get to know your target audiences. You can find out what people think about your site, product or service.
- Prevent crises. By looking out for mentions of your business, you will be able to correct misinformation and quell rumours.
- Conduct competitor research (see above).
- Analyse consumer trends. By keeping track of relevant discussion groups, you will be able to predict consumer trends that could affect your business.

The quickest and easiest way to research discussion groups is via the Deja News search service (http://www.dejanews.com). You can search individual discussion groups or the entire database at once (see Figure 3.3).

Conduct research from your site

One of the most effective ways to evaluate your e-PR success is to use your site as a research aid. People who visit your site are, by definition, members of your core target audience and information on them can therefore help you focus your e-PR strategy.

There are a number of ways you can use your site to find out more about your online audience.

- Ask people to subscribe to an online newsletter or e-zine. Getting people to subscribe to something can be a great way of obtaining information such as e-mail addresses.
- Ask for customer feedback at your site. Use e-mail links or feedback forms to collect feedback, comments and queries from site visitors.

E-mail research

E-mail can be a useful way of conducting primary market research online. Once you have built up a list of e-mail addresses from your site, you can send out survey questionnaires. To avoid annoying

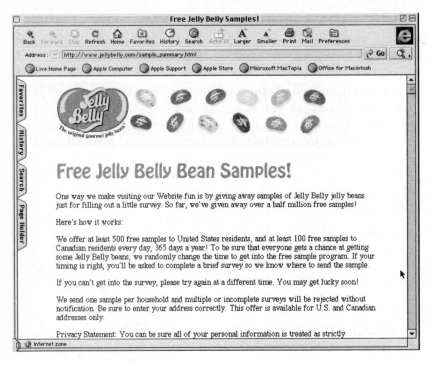

Figure 3.4 The Jelly Belly Web site is regularly used for market research purposes

people on your mailing list you could attach questionnaires to your online newsletter rather than send them out independently.

When you are sending questionnaires to lots of different e-mail addresses at the same time, use the Bcc: (Blind Carbon Copy) function to keep each e-mail address invisible to the recipients. Here are some tips on putting together an online questionnaire:

- Keep each question short and easy to understand.
- Put an HTML link to your site at the foot of the questionnaire. This way even if people do not fill in the questionnaire they can make a repeat visit to your site.
- Use a multiple choice format.
- If you want your research to be broken down into figures and percentages, a multiple choice is preferable to an open answer format. Multiple choice also makes it easier for the recipient, and therefore means it is more likely that the questionnaire will be completed and returned.
- Offer an incentive. To ensure that the questionnaire is completed and returned, offer a gift or prize to the people who complete it. Jelly Belly (http://www.jellybelly.com) offered customers free Jelly Belly beans for this purpose (see Figure 3.4).

Use research findings to generate publicity

Research not only helps you plan your e-PR campaigns; it can also be a source of PR itself. One of the more effective ways of generating publicity is to conduct research and release your findings. Research relating to online activity is particularly valuable to the media as it helps feed an ever-growing public interest in the Internet. The Internet is a new medium that is developing at an unprecedented rate. As such, statistics and percentages relating to the Internet appear on an almost daily basis in the national newspapers and in TV news and consumer programmes. Companies such as Yahoo!, Amazon.com, AOL, Netscape, Demon and Excite use research as a publicity tool to great effect, publishing research findings and survey results on a regular basis.

Out of all Internet-related features in the media, research-based stories prove to be among the most frequent. This is illustrated by looking at the news sections of Internet magazines that are permeated with research-led stories. The following article in *.net* magazine is typical of the way research is used to generate media interest:

Knickers to all that

Research from Intel in the UK has shown that only 10 per cent of men from the South East would buy lingerie online purely to avoid the embarrassment of making high street purchases, compared to 46 per cent of males surveyed in the South West and Wales. The same survey also stated that nine out of ten women agreed that parents should understand the technology they are using.

Intel's research has a media interest because it combines gender and geographic differences. The following extracts are all further examples of how research can gain publicity (taken from *Internet.Works* magazine):

- Brits love Net Shopping: New Research from Visa has highlighted the uptake of e-commerce in the UK.
- Europeans set to shop online: E-retailers must prepare for growth in European e-commerce says survey.
- AOL recently release usage figures: Nearly one third (29%) use the service every day of the week. . .
- Vital Statistics: According to Online Agency research, Explorer dominates the browser market. . .
- Women on the Net: Every month 150,000 new women come online.

To generate your own headlines in the media, you should think about how to put a media friendly spin on your research findings. There are certain Internet research topics that are particularly welcomed by journalists and editors. Here are some of them:

- Gender. Research concerning the ratio of male to female Internet users is a continual hot topic.
- Internet versus TV. The level of Internet usage compared with TV and other offline media has been examined in a variety of surveys and continues to generate coverage.
- The popularity of niche markets. If you have a niche interest site, research confirming a large number of visitors can be of media interest. The online delicatessen Teddington Cheese

(http://www. Teddingtoncheese.co.uk) is one niche site that has gained press coverage in this way.

- The Internet's effect on 'real world' activity. Research into how the Internet can change 'real world' habits and behaviour is valued by journalists and editors.

Summary

Researching audiences online helps you to direct and target e-PR activity. The Internet is a great research tool as it enables you to conduct both secondary research (via search engines) and primary research (by communicating to your audiences directly). Furthermore, online research can be a source of publicity in itself, feeding the media's craving for Internet-based facts and figures. The most valuable form of research will therefore be that which provides you with a valuable insight into your online public while generating publicity at the same time.

four

Web **site basics**

For all the books out there on the technical aspects of Web site design, there is a manifest lack of material exploring the more fundamental principle of what makes a Web site an effective communication tool. This may explain, partly at least, why there are so many technically competent sites out there either attracting no visitors at all or the wrong type of visitor. This chapter seeks to even the balance a little by looking at the basics of effective relations-building Web sites.

Identify your site objectives

Every e-business will have different objectives for its site. These objectives will clearly depend on whether it has an e-commerce or support site. However, there are some common objectives for all business sites wanting to conduct effective e-PR:

- to attract new visitors;
- to build relations with existing visitors;
- to generate repeat traffic;
- to involve the visitor;
- to appeal to visitors relevant to your business.

As well as these general aims, you need to determine the specific objectives you want your site to achieve (advice on formulating objectives is provided in Chapter 2).

Wrong reasons to have a site

There are many reasons why people decide to have a Web site. Most of them, however, centre on a misinterpretation of what the Internet can and should provide its users. Here is what seems to go through the heads of many business owners deciding to get a site:

- 'Everyone else has one, why shouldn't I?'
- 'This site will blow people away with my artistic brilliance.'
- 'I want my site to be the Sistine Chapel of the Internet age!'
- 'I will use our company brochure as the basis of our site.'
- 'Let's register our domain name and then put an 'under construction' sign up. At least then we can put our site address on our stationery.'
- 'Having a Web site is a sure-fire way to get rich. We'll be able to get venture capital and float on the stock market within three weeks. Ha, Ha!'

If your thoughts are even close to *any* of the above, you are not going to end up with an effective site. Whether your objective is to have an e-commerce site that sells your products and services online, or to have a brand-building site that supports offline activity, you need to think in terms of e-PR. Your site needs to help you to start and consolidate relations that will aid the development of your business. To have a site which works for you also needs to work for its visitors.

The domain name game

The first impression a visitor has of your Web site is formed by its address or URL (Uniform Resource Locator). Before an Internet user sees your home page, he or she will have to see or type your site address. Contrary to what a lot of people clearly think, not all URLs are equal. Consider the following two addresses:

1. http://www.ourworld.compuserve.com/homepages/chocoholic
2. http://www.chocoholic.com

Number one is an example of a site set up with a free service (in this case CompuServe). Number two is a site that has registered its own domain name ('chocoholic') so it doesn't have to use anyone else's. The number two site clearly forms a better impression, and gets its site–visitor relations off to a better start. It looks more professional, is easier to remember and is more likely to get you on the major search engines. It is therefore essential to register your own domain name if you are to make the right impact on your target audiences. Furthermore, using a free service doesn't save you that much money as you can register your own domain for as little as $70 in the US and £50 in the UK.

The other point to remember with domain names is that you should always use the name of your company where possible. It may also be a good idea to register a relevant generic term as a domain name (one site can have various domain names simultaneously). For instance, Ragu has two URLs: http://www.ragu.com as well as http://www.eat.com that it uses for different marketing purposes (see Figure 4.1).

The second part of a domain name (after the dot), known as a top-level domain (TLD), also warrants some careful consideration. If you want to attract a nation-specific audience, you should use a

Figure 4.1 Ragu's site has two different Web site addresses

nation-specific TLD such as -.co.uk. If you are an organization or public service, you could use -.net or -.org as your TLD. In most instances, however, -.com is your best option as it is what visitors will automatically type unless they already know otherwise.

Download times

Another factor that affects the visitor's first impression of your Web site is the length of time your site takes to be downloaded. If your page takes longer than ten seconds to download, impatient visitors will end the site–visitor relationship there and then. If the total combined file size (including the HTML, graphics and so on) is over 40k, you can assume your site will lose visitors. Therefore, a site with minimal text and graphics on its home page will be quicker to download.

Love at first site

E-PR is not just concerned with getting people to your site; it is about building relations when they get there. You can get thousands of hits a day, but if people are bored when they get there, you are clearly not going to get what you want from your site.

The next thing you need to consider is the initial impression the site itself makes on a new visitor. You have to make sure your home page makes an impact. You have no more than, say, 15 seconds before your visitor asks the age-old question, 'Should I stay or should I go?' Your e-PR is not effective if they choose to leave, as 15-second relationships are not good for your business. You need to grab their interest on the first page, and then move them along.

Navigation

Simple and straightforward navigation is a fundamental rule of Web site e-PR. If it takes a lot of effort to explore the different sections of your site, visitors will not return. On vast e-commerce and information-rich sites, navigation is even more of an issue as the more products or information you offer, the harder it can be for visitors to find what they want. You must therefore find a way to make the site easy for your visitors to move around in. Here are some guidelines to help keep Web site navigation simple:

- **Don't go link crazy.** Too many navigation links can be as frustrating as too few. If you've got more than 10 links – and on a menu page that is quite probable – divide them into groups of 10 or less.
- **Tell people where they are.** If possible, try to give your visitors some indication of their bearings. You can do this by providing a site map or by changing the colour of the current section in the navigation area.
- **Have a neat and tidy structure.** If your site structure is a mess, your navigation will be messy too. Make sure your structure is adapted to accommodate new sections and changes to your site, as new additions are the main causes of messy navigation problems.
- **Obey the 'three click' rule.** The 'three click' rule states that no page of your site should be any more than three clicks away from another.
- **Make links clear.** 'Home', 'News', 'Contact', 'Product Information', 'Help' and 'About This Site' may seem slightly dull titles for links but they will make sense to your visitor and avoid confusion. If you want to use your site to express your verbal ingenuity, your link titles are not the place to do it. Don't be afraid to use the straightforward command 'Click Here' as a request for action.
- **Keep links central.** Keeping links in the centre of the page means visitors won't need to scroll down or across to reach them.
- **Link every page.** Make sure every page has at least one navigation link. The search engines will bring visitors straight to pages deep in your site, so make every page an acceptable starting point. Most pages have a link to the home page, the head of the current section, and a handful of other section heads, but you don't have to follow this format religiously.
- **Never rely on the Back Button for navigation.** If visitors who have reached your site via a search engine are encouraged to use the Back button, they will end up going back to the search engine they came from.

- **Be constant.** Include the same navigation bar and graphic buttons on each page. This will make pages quicker to load and keep things simple for your visitors. Making navigation easy will help convey a good image of the company as well as improve the experience for the visitor.
- **Make your site's navigation work for you.** While making sure that your site is easy to use for your visitors, your navigation also needs to work for you. For instance, if you want to tell people about your online newsletter you need to make sure they pass that information en route to where they want to get to.

Writing on the Web

The Internet is essentially a text-based medium. The way you write on your Web site therefore affects the way the business is viewed by your online visitors. Furthermore, the experience of reading information on the Internet is completely different to that of reading a newspaper, a company brochure or other printed material. For this reason, writing on the Web needs to be treated from a different perspective.

When writing text for your Web site you need to take the following facts into consideration:

- People get bored easily. Goldfish are said to have a five-second attention span. That is approximately two seconds more than most Web users. If they are visiting your site via a search engine, they probably have a list of at least 10 other sites they want to visit.
- Reading large chunks of text on an electronic monitor tends to cause eyestrain and fatigue.
- Most people use the Internet for e-mail purposes. They have therefore come to associate online text with informality.
- The majority of Web sites written in English originate from the United States. US spellings and colloquialisms are therefore the norm.
- Unlike books and other printed media, people don't put a Web site down halfway through reading it and then come back to finish it off later. On the Web, you only have one short chance to make an impression.

With these facts in mind you need to make sure that your text is:

- **Easy to read.** Black text on a light background is ideal. Break up text by putting spaces around paragraphs.
- **Short, snappy and to the point.** Information fatigue is the enemy of good online relations. George Orwell's classic advice to prefer the short word to the long holds true for writing on the Web.
- **Informal and personal.** Avoid cold, formal language. Informal text makes your business seem more accessible and welcoming.
- **Spelt correctly.** Stick to US spellings if you seek to cater for an international audience.

It is also a good idea to have a short sentence on your home page stating clearly what the site is about. Furthermore, when writing text for your site remember that your visitor wants to know what's in it for him or her. Therefore, write about the benefits that your site provides its audiences. If you keep this in mind as you write your site you are halfway to e-PR success already.

If you still find that you struggle in your search for Web words that work, visit Quoteland (http://www.quoteland.com) where Net-friendly sound bites and quotes can be searched and browsed by theme.

A site for sore eyes

The usual design of your Web site needs to be well thought out if you are to communicate your business message effectively. The design of your site will affect the way that visitors respond. Good design makes information more likely to be read and the site easier to navigate.

- Avoid using too many graphic images as they take longer to download than text. Small images are easier to download than large images.
- **Make your design relevant** to your target audiences. Think about the type of magazines your visitors read as well as what other sites they visit for inspiration.
- **Keep sites clean.** A busy, multi-coloured site will end up giving your visitor a headache and detracting from your message.

Cleaner sites with a minimal and coherent use of colour make a better psychological impression. Stick to two or three dominant colours.

- **Don't use dark or two-tone backgrounds.** Dark and multi-coloured interfaces can make text difficult to decipher. There are some colour combinations that work well on the Web, however. Gold on blue or red on green, for instance, provide a high level of contrast and can therefore be used for text/background combinations.
- **Use the right font.** Whereas in the real world you can get away with using whatever font you want, on the Web there are definitely some that work better. The most popular 'real world' font, Times Roman, does not transfer that well to the Web. Its complex little flourishes (serifs) are lost on Web pages. Verdana is generally considered the easiest font to read on the Web, as it was specifically designed for that exact purpose. Simple, unfussy fonts such as Arial, Georgia and Helvetica also work particularly well on Web sites and are proving increasingly popular.
- **Use different font sizes.** Make headings, sub-headings and key phrases a different (bigger) size to the standard text.
- **Form follows function.** When you have a site that works you can then start to make it look visually attractive. Where a compromise situation is required, you should remember that it is more important that your site works and is easy to navigate than that it looks good.

The trick is to keep your site simple enough to appeal to new visitors and stimulating enough to keep old ones coming back.

Make your site 'sticky'

When a visitor has found your site, you want him or her to stay there as long as possible. To do this you will need to make your site so 'sticky' (as Net heads call it) that visitors will be reluctant to leave. To make your site more 'sticky' you could do one or more of the following:

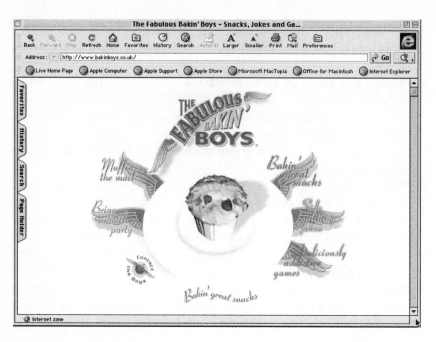

Figure 4.2 The Fabulous Bakin'Boys site

▨ Provide a large amount of rich and relevant information spread out over many pages (too much text on a single page puts your visitors off).

▨ Make it highly interactive (see the next chapter).

▨ Put a bulletin board on your site (as opposed to a discussion area which tends to draw people away from the heart of your site).

▨ Make sure any links to other sites are as far away from your home page as possible.

Site close-up

The Fabulous Bakin' Boys (http://www.muffinthemil.co.uk)

The site of muffin-maker extraordinaire, The Fabulous Bakin' Boys, is a very 'sticky' site due to its creative and playful use of interactivity. On arrival at the home page the visitor can link to one of the following sections:

- 'Bakin' great snacks' – the TFBB product range.
- 'Side-splitting jokes' – the site encourages visitors to send in their favourite jokes.
- 'Deliciously addictive games' – Interactive games help keep visitors at their site. This section also includes a quiz about morality.
- 'Muffin the Mail' – extracts from visitors' e-mail messages.
- 'Bring a Bottle Party' – this section is the highlight of the site. It simulates an aspect of the real world that its visitors can relate to (a house party) and provides relevant information (for example a selection of cocktail recipes) (see Figure 4.2).

Building trust on your site

Online or offline, strong relationships depend on trust. The trouble with the Internet is that, despite its rapidly growing popularity, many people are often not willing to place their trust in online businesses. This suspicion of e-business is, at least partly, justified. The fact that the Internet lowers the barriers of entry into the international market place means that virtually anyone and his or her dog can set up shop online. As a result, many unscrupulous e-businesses out there are exploiting the Internet's relative lack of regulation and giving e-business as a whole a bad name.

Furthermore, the volatility of dot com companies on the stock market has also added to the sense of mistrust of e-business in general and e-commerce sites in particular.

There are, however, a number of proactive ways you can combat any suspicions your visitors may have and build beneficial relations based on trust:

- **Register your own domain name**. As mentioned previously, this is essential for a business site to make the right psychological impression. Having the URL http://www.geocities.com/ Barcelona/FirstQuarter/56492/mysite.com or anything of similar length, which indicates you are using a free service, will do little to build trust. Registering your own domain gives the impression that you are here to stay.

- **Place all your contact details on the site**. Names, phone numbers and a real world address help to instil confidence in your site because it means people know where to find you if something goes wrong.
- **Put faces to the company**. Putting pictures of you, your colleagues or employees on your site with a brief and informal CV gives people a clearer 'real world' picture of your business.
- **Ensure visitors that their contact details will remain confidential.** If you have an area of your site that visitors need to register for to enter, you need to make clear that you will not sell their details to mailing list companies. This applies equally to online newsletter subscriptions and anywhere that encourages e-mail or form-based feedback.
- **Use a Secure Server**. If you have an e-commerce site and plan to take orders online, you will need a secure server. This will make sure credit card transactions remain secure. Credit card details typed into an order form will then be encrypted before being sent from the visitor's browser to the Web server to take online orders. Many people will be deterred from placing orders if you decide not to.
- **Add a sense of history**. Businesses that have been around a while are more likely to generate a sense of trust than businesses set up five weeks ago. However, Internet time moves faster than real time and if a site has been set up for more than a couple of years it can be considered to have a substantial online heritage. If your business has operated offline for a number of years but is relatively new to cyberspace, emphasize your 'real world' history on your site. Mention when you were established and, if appropriate, include a 'company history' page on your site. If you have been set up for a really long time you could incorporate old black and white photographs and other company memorabilia onto your site. Marks and Spencer (http://www.marksandspencer.com) and The Whisky Shop (http://www.thewhiskyshop.com) make good and prominent use of old photographs on their sites.

Cyber suspense

To keep people at your site, and to keep them coming back, you may need an element of suspense. Your site should be in people's minds between visits, so that when they do need your product or service they know where to turn. There are many ways to make your site the online equivalent of a page turner people don't want to put down and can't wait to get back to:

- **Have a 'What's New' section.** Make sure virgin visitors realize that your site is regularly updated by providing a 'What's New' or 'Site News' page.
- **Put a soap opera on your site.** Ragu's 'Eat as the Lasagne Bakes' soap (http://www.eat.com) has a loyal fan base of regular visitors who e-mail storyline suggestions. Some business sites now even include online 'docu-soaps' 'starring' the company's staff. On some sites, people can watch developments in real time via a Web-cam. This may be a way of keeping your more voyeuristic visitors coming back.
- **Order information in a series.** Rather than revealing everything at once, you should give information away in stages. One particularly successful formula involves running online tutorials over a number of weeks on a topic relevant to your business.
- **Put a small amount of text on your home page.** Have just enough text on your home page to give visitors an idea of what's inside, but put large amounts of information at least two links away.

Summary

For a Web site to work it needs to boost your reputation by building relationships with relevant audiences. To do this effectively you need to make sure that your site is user-friendly and that it is trusted. It also needs to be equally stimulating for site virgins and veterans alike. This means a straightforward navigation alongside well thought out text and design.

As well as being user-friendly, however, your site also needs to build trust and respect. The next chapter will look at further ways to build valuable relations via your site by capitalizing on the Internet's most significant characteristic, interactivity.

five

Get **interactive**

Effective PR is based on good relationships and good relationships are based on interactivity. Indeed, it is the process of interaction that actually *defines* a relationship. The Internet is the perfect medium to build relationships because it allows and encourages interactivity. Whereas television only offers the *viewer* a limited opportunity to interact (to switch on and off or change channels), the Internet *user* can have a more interactive role to play. To have a site that provides you with successful e-PR you must capitalize on this and make it highly interactive.

Interactive Web sites are two-way, not one-way communication tools; they encourage dialogue and conversation between your target audiences and your company. A static company brochure transferred to cyberspace simply will not work. Companies must take advantage of, and use to their full potential, the interactive and multimedia tools that are available on the market today. The most successful sites, from Amazon to Yahoo!, all have one thing in common: they build relationships with their target audiences by encouraging two-way interaction. This will ensure visitors enjoy your site and keep returning. This chapter therefore looks at the various ways you can capture the imagination of your visitors by adding interactive elements to your site.

'Itchy finger' syndrome

As we have discussed earlier, people tend to have a very short attention span when surfing the Net. The fact is that when people log online they expect their fingers to be kept busy; they do not expect to sit passively at a computer screen reading limitless amounts of text.

The more visitors can actively use their mouse and keyboard at your site, the more they are going to be interested in what's happening on the monitor. You therefore need to assume that most of your audience will be afflicted by 'itchy finger' syndrome, the main symptom of which is an overbearing desire to click on a mouse at least once every fifteen seconds. If they cannot do this at your site, they will not hesitate to go elsewhere. One of the most effective ways of keeping itchy fingers busy is to add a form to your site.

Add forms to your site

You can add a form to your site to encourage comments, criticisms, queries and orders, providing you keep it simple and easy to understand. It is often a good idea to have different forms for different audiences. For instance, you could have an order form on one page, a customer questionnaire on another and a form that allows journalists to ask for information or review products on another. Adding a form is relatively straightforward, especially if you use one of the more recent Web site design programs such as Dreamweaver, Microsoft Front Page or Adobe Page Mill that enable you to add and adapt form templates. When the page is designed, you will require a 'Perl' script that runs on your Web server to manage the response and the distribution of the form's contents. However, if this seems a little intimidating, you can receive a ready-made script from your Internet Service Provider (ISP) to automate this process.

Some Web sites ask users to complete a registration form before they enter a site or receive a free download. If you do this, remember not to ask for too much information – the last thing you want to do is deter customers from entering or returning to the site.

Forms tend to use a selection or combination of the following features:

- **Text boxes.** As you would probably expect, text boxes enable visitors to type information into a box. The text box is defined by the number of characters that fit into the box width. An asterisk will appear when any key is pressed in a password text box.

- **Radio buttons.** Radio buttons are often used at the end of a form to give users the choice of whether they want to receive information about related products/services or to be excluded from mailing lists. Users can choose one selection from a list on the screen.
- **Drop down boxes.** A drop down box allows users to choose one selection from a list that 'drops down' when the relevant option is chosen. This tool is a useful space saver as the lists only appear on screen when the drop down arrow is clicked. If you include drop down buttons, remember the 'other' option – not all customers will fit into defined categories. Drop down buttons, as a norm, only allow one answer to be chosen but multiple choices can be set (ensure that your multiple option drop down list is compatible with all servers and also that clear usage instructions are provided on the form).
- **Check boxes.** A check box is used when a user is given a choice of more than one answer from a given set.
- **Submit buttons.** Submit buttons are normally situated at the bottom of the form (most likely with the word 'submit' written on them). When the user clicks the submit button, the information on the form is automatically sent to the Web server for processing.
- **Clear buttons.** Clear buttons are usually placed alongside the submit button. A clear button enables a visitor to erase everything he or she has written on a form in order to start again. Try not to place the submit and clear button too close together for obvious reasons.

As indicated above, online forms must be concise and clear to all your audiences. For example, remember to include a ZIP code/postal code box rather than just one or the other when targeting the UK and the United States. Confusing your customer will not lead to a harmonious online relationship.

The most basic form would include a comments box and send button; however, much more creative and complex forms can be utilized to create a longer-lasting impact.

While the information on, say, a feedback form is simple to process (all the information is e-mailed to the Web site administrator), online shopping forms are slightly more complex as the user has to select items and then add them to an online shopping basket. The order information that must be displayed on the e-commerce forms includes lists of products on sale, quantities required, delivery and payment details. Furthermore, they require complex computer programs that will include the database of the product information, price per product and quantity in stock. Amazon's near-legendary order form has a user-friendly structure and makes an essentially complex process look straightforward.

Personal automatic response 'thank you' pages can be set up. This means that, when a user forwards his or her request, message or order, he or she will receive a personalized message in return, as opposed to an impersonal and over formal 'to: Sir/Madam'. This simple gesture will help make your customers feel that little bit closer to the site.

On top of all these practical considerations, you also need to be creative in your use of forms. To make sure your form generates a good response you need to use your imagination. For instance, on a feedback form instead of asking people to respond on a scale of one to five, you might want to inject life to your form by displaying a sense of humour. This is what Wine Cellar (http://www.wine-cellar.com) has done on its site. To give you a flavour of their highly successful questionnaire form, here is one of its multiple-choice questions:

Q:Overall, do you find the site easy to use?

A:1. Woof!

2. Considering that I was also feeding the baby, cooking dinner and chatting to Claire. . . not bad at all.

3. Easier than penetrating vacuum packed bacon, but only a touch.

4. Years of setting video recorders helped me through.

5. Fortunately, Carol Vorderman is staying with us.

By making your forms and questionnaires easy and entertaining to read, you will strengthen relations at the same time as you conduct valuable research.

Add a guest book

One of the most basic ways of encouraging your guests to interact with your company is to provide a guest book. Guest books work particularly well for sites with small and geographically spread out audiences. Users can write their comments about your site to share with you and other visitors. A guest book serves a similar function as a bulletin board system (used for newsgroups) but is significantly simpler to install and operate. Your ISP will be able to provide you with a script you can use. If not, visit Freecode (http://www.freecode.com) for a range of free packages that you can put on your Web server.

Hold an online auction

If you have an e-commerce site, one interesting and unique possibility you have open to you is to hold an online auction. Believe it or not, online auctions constitute the fastest growing segment of the entire e-commerce market. As e-PR is about building mutually beneficial relationships, the online auction is perfect as both you and your customer will benefit. One of the biggest online auctions can be found at http://www.qxl.com.

As well as strengthening customer–site relations, there are several other reasons why you might decide to hold an online auction:

- Auctions help you decide the best fixed price for new products.
- They can bring a new audience to your site.
- They are a media-friendly way of gaining online and offline publicity.
- They can provide visitors with 24-hour access to products and services.

There are two types of online auction – the first is where the products are controlled by the Web site (check out http://www.iflybritish.com – where British Midlands auction seats – see Figure 5.1); the other can be defined as an online flea market. The online flea market allows users to buy and sell products on the site but the Web site holds no responsibility. E Bay and Yahoo! Auctions are good examples. Online flea markets provide chat rooms for potential buyers and sellers to discuss the products.

The types of products that have previously sold well on online auctions include:

- theatre and concert tickets;
- holidays;

Figure 5.1 British Midlands auction seats on their Web site

- IT products;
- antiques;
- memorabilia;
- houses.

The growing demand for online auctions has led to much auction software programming being developed by companies such as Opensite (http://www.opensite.com) and Instil (http://www. Instil.com).

Key features included on most auction software are:

- news boards with vendor and purchaser feedback, which are fully searchable and indexed;
- keyword profiling to help organize products placed for auction;
- live currency and exchange rate translators allowing visitors to view prices in multiple currencies.

Online auctions normally follow this pattern:

- Products are shown on the auctioneer's site.
- Auction schedules are set and promoted.
- Bidders log onto the site, normally registering and submitting a credit card number.
- Bidders bid for goods by clicking a Bid button (it is usual on auction sites for no bid to be valid unless accompanied by a password).
- Without the aid of a hammer and an auctioneer's cry of 'Going, going, gone', the final bid is worked out in one of two ways: either at a set closing time or a set amount of time after a new bid.
- The successful bidder is notified by e-mail with all the relevant instructions and delivery details.

Coupons

Online coupons can be installed on your Web site and customers can download the relevant coupons, print them out and receive a discount. There are coupon sites such as http://www.ecoupons.com and http://www.coolsavings.com where you can place your own coupons on their sites and users search for coupons by their area of interest. To find a list of coupon sites go to Yahoo! then click to the following sections: Business and Economy, Companies, Marketing, Advertising and Coupons.

E-mailing lists

Ask visitors to join your e-mailing list and then send e-mails notifying them of new articles and offerings at your site. The benefits of this are twofold as it will encourage repeat traffic to your site and help you identify strong prospects. Remember to clarify that all e-mail addresses will remain confidential.

You can manage your own mailing list by saving all your mailing list subscribers in an address book in your e-mail program. You have to add and delete subscribers manually; that may be time consuming depending on the size of your mailing list. Some programs conveniently handle your mailing list for you, Eudora Pro for example. Others will host your mailing list for free, such as Ergots (http://www.egroups.com) and One List (http://www.onelist.com). They advertise on your mailing list for free in return for their services. Alternatively or alongside your mailing list, you can offer subscription to a newsletter (either your own or one relating to your area of business).

Have a 'Q and A' page

Encourage visitors to e-mail questions relating to your company and get an expert (either you or an employee) to provide informative and entertaining answers. This relationship-building tactic can lead to you and your company eventually becoming an authority on your business area. Remember to update the section regularly and keep online archives of the most common questions and answers for visitors to browse through.

It's a good idea to include the name of the person who asks the question and the company to add authenticity. Be honest with your answers and try not to plug your company too much (think of it more as what marketing boffins might term 'subliminal persuasion through association'). Site visitors want answers to questions, not blatant promotion.

Sell products and services online

Another way of creating an interactive site is by selling products and services online. Strong relationships can be built if the e-commerce process provides the customer with a rewarding experience. You will require a customer shopping system to sell goods online.

Keep the customer updated with the process of the order and ensure that you:

- send an e-mail message confirming the order and quoting an order number to the customer;
- send an e-mail message confirming authorization and delivery dates;
- deliver the goods on time.

Customer satisfaction is the key to e-commerce success. If an e-commerce site is not handled correctly, it takes one angry customer minutes to vent his or her dissatisfaction in front of hundreds of online discussion groups. The e-commerce sites that make the grade (from Amazon down) make sure the customer is made to feel important rather than an expendable market unit.

For more information on creating a relation-building e-commerce site, visit the following Yahoo! addresses:

- Yahoo! – Electronic Commerce –
  http://www.yahoo.com/Business_and_Economy/Electronic_Commerce/;
- Yahoo! – Electronic Commerce Software –
  http://www.yahoo.com/Business_and_Economy/Companies/Retail_Management_Supplies_and_Services/Electronic_Commerce/Software/

Also, check out Sell It On The Web – http://www.SellItOnTheWeb.com, which shares a veritable goldmine of information on how to set up an e-commerce site (see Figure 5.2).

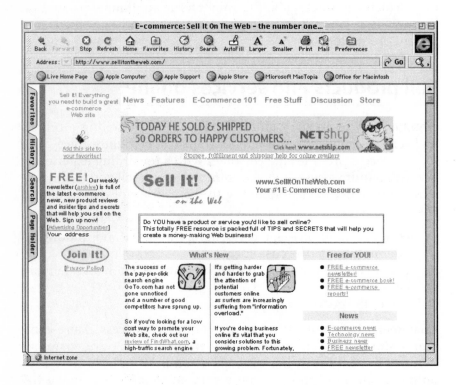

Figure 5.2 Sell It On The Web provides a lot of information on how to set up an e-commerce site

Encourage your visitors to send you articles and features

Encourage your visitors to provide you with site content. The popular Web site entitled 'Web Sites That Suck' (http://www. Websitesthatsuck.com) is based on this concept (see Figure 5.3). Readers submit to the site's administrator Web sites that they believe 'suck', along with their personal critiques. This provides the administrator with the majority of the material for the site while at the same time strengthening the site's bond with its online audiences. Some of your visitors will be more than willing to write online articles and features if they are interested in your Web site content.

Figure 5.3 Web sites that Suck is a popular Web site

Hold regular and imaginative competitions relevant to your business

Competitions are a great e-PR weapon in the battle for improved site–visitor relations. Make sure your competitions are as relevant as possible to your target audience. Amazon holds regular competitions where a famous author writes a first chapter and visitors are invited to write the second.

Site close-up

Country bookstore – http://www.countrybookstore.co.uk

The Country Bookstore site builds customer relations through a high level of interactivity. It has a 'Top 100 Books and Authors' section where visitors can cast a vote. There's also a monthly prize quiz where users can test their literary knowledge.

Offer something for free download or access

This could include free download, access, trials, samples or consultations. To use this technique to build strong relationships you need to ensure 'freebies' are valuable and helpful to the user while making sure that the user will still require your services. Ensure you can meet demand for the freebies and take into account delivery expenses (if a product is involved) – one free T-shirt per customer could leave you bankrupt. Companies that provide freebies as part of their e-PR efforts include Adobe (http://www.adobe.com) that offers free downloads on their Web site and JellyBelly (http://www.jellybelly.com) that offers free samples of their product.

Put a search engine on your site

If your site is large enough to justify it, put a search engine on, using the free downloadable search software at Softsearch (http://www.softsearch.com). A search engine tool increases customer satisfaction by facilitating navigation on a site and providing users with easy access to all the information they require.

Waitrose (http://www.waitrose.co.uk) is one company that uses a search engine in an innovative way. On the Waitrose site visitors choose a meal type (eg breakfast), a preparation time (eg 20 minutes) and ingredients they plan to use (eg bacon and eggs). The search engine then displays recipes that match the criteria they have chosen.

Personalize your site

Interactivity enables you to personalize information in a way that traditional promotional media, such as a company brochure or printed newsletter, cannot. To personalize your site:

- Provide an online 'help line' allowing customers, journalists and 'just passing through' casual visitors to ask a question relating to your business that you will respond to within a stated time frame.
- Offer free online one-to-one consultations from your site.
- Thank people for comments about your site and personalize the message.
- Respond to any enquiries as quickly as possible and personalize them.
- Divide your site into different sections relating to different target audiences (customers, journalists, etc).

Provide links

Links (also known as hyperlinks) provide users with the ability to navigate through a Web site and link to related sites. Most Web sites have links that connect one location on the site to another (even links that jump within the page) and links to e-mail addresses (place these in your contact area). Linkage buttons do not have to be only text; they can also be graphics files.

While most people appreciate the value of having a link *to* your site, many do not realize it can be worthwhile having links *from* your site as well. Although links offer people an open doorway to leave your site, visitors welcome a resource page that includes links to useful and related sites. The fact is that people are going to leave your site anyway, and adding a links page is more likely to encourage repeat traffic than lose you visitors. Think of a link as another reason for people to come to your site, rather than as an excuse to leave. You can also involve visitors in your use of links by asking them to submit their suggestions for appropriate sites they have linked on their Net travels.

Furthermore, there is another way that links away from your site can serve your own ends. For instance, Riverside Foods (http://www.riversidefoods.com) provides a link to a hotel restaurant that is supplied by Riverside's products. Wine Cellar (http://www.winecellar.com) is another example of a site that uses links in a relevant and effective way. It has an astonishing 52 links to related wine sites, providing its audiences with information they cannot attain from their own site.

In order to try and build up reciprocal links to your Web site, you could research the following:

- The link lists of other relevant sites.
- Web rings (they provide links from one site in a group to other sites): see Web ring (http://www.Webring.org), Loop link (http://www. looplink.com) and The Rail (http://www. therail.com).
- Link Exchange Services (they link relevant Web sites to one another). For instance, check out Missing Link (http:// www./goldrush.com/ missing).

Add multimedia

Add live sound and videos to your Web site to heighten the impact of a visit. Multimedia servers that support audio and video include:

- RealMedia – http://www.realaudio.com;
- StreamWorks – http://www.xingtech.com;
- VDO Live – http://www.vdo.com.

Provide translations

The aim of e-PR is to build relationships with all of your online audiences. If your market expands beyond English speaking countries, keep this in mind by providing language translations for your site. Translation agencies can be found at Yahoo! under the section 'Languages: translations'.

In addition, you might consider registering a local domain name such as 'au' for Australia and 'fr' for France – check with your service provider for country-specific domains. Remember to check which computer systems are the preferred choice in the country you are targeting; for example, in France the Apple Macintosh is dominant whereas in the United States it's the PC.

Create a community

If you want to make sure visitors return to your site on a regular basis, you need to create a strong sense of community. If you can make people feel as if they *belong* to your site, you will consequently find it easier to generate loyalty among your target audiences. Ways to create a community include:

- **Registration.** Making people register to enter your site is one way to enhance customer loyalty. If you feel this may deter people from visiting your site in the first instance, you could designate a certain area of your site as a registration area, instead of the whole site. London nightclub and record label, Ministry of Sound (http://www.ministryofsound.com), have done this with their 'VIP Room', a registration-only area which entitles visitors to pick up exclusive information unavailable elsewhere on the site (see Figure 5.4).

Remember that if you are intending people to register for your site or a section of it, there must be a sufficient incentive for them to do

Figure 5.4 Ministry of Sound offer VIP benefits on their Web site

so; you need to provide exclusive information of genuine value to them. Furthermore, you must make clear that any information your visitors give you will remain secure and not be sold to market research or direct e-mail companies. Most recent Web-building programs, such as all versions of Dreamweaver, enable you to add registration forms and access facilities to your existing site.

■ **Replicate the real word.** Many sites that have built successful and mutually beneficial relations with their visitors have done so by replicating aspects of real world communities. The most obvious example is the GeoCities site (http://www.geocities.com) which links different sites together to create online towns and shopping malls. People like a point of reference they can relate to the world of bricks and mortar. That is why a 'chat **room**' is more evocative than a 'chat **area**', and an 'online **office**' sometimes sounds better than 'our company **Web site**'.

■ **Add a discussion group.** Discussion groups enable your visitors to air their feelings to other members of your audience. Discussion groups are similar to guest books but messages on discussion groups can be **threaded** (where the message and the reply are shown together). It's a useful way of keeping up-to-date with what your visitors' opinions are (see the chapter on discussion groups for a more in-depth analysis of the topic).

Sites that provide consumers with the ability to interact with one another, in addition to the company, can help build new and deeper site–visitor relations. The Wine Cellar site (http://www.winecellar.com) does this to great effect through its 'Wine Cellar Arena' that enables visitors to leave messages, comments or to e-mail other users (see Figure 5.5).

■ **Add a bulletin board.** This works in the same way as a bulletin board works in the real world. Messages are posted on the board for everyone to see. The two main advantages of the bulletin board system are that your visitors interact with one another and therefore they stay on your site. Bulletin board software can be found at http://www.freecode.com (a total of 500 programs can be found here).

Figure 5.5 The Wine Cellar Arena encourages interactivity

■ **Add chat and conferencing facilities.** Online chat conferencing facilities can add pulling power to your site to attract your various audiences. The opportunities chat rooms offer are immense. Examples include live guest appearances with a technical guru, live press conferences and live business meetings.

There are essentially two ways groups of people can communicate on the Internet – via online chat and conferencing systems. They can 'chat' live (Real Time Chat) or read and respond later (Asynchronous Chat) via text, voice and video.

In chat areas, visitors are not referred to by either name or e-mail address as they are in mailing lists and newsgroups; instead they generally choose a 'nickname'.

Interactive real time chat requires software to set up the rooms. Software that is tailored for this role includes Ichat (http://www.ichat.com), Proxicom (http://www.proxicom.com) and ChatWare (http://www.eware.com).

Be creative

Be creative and keep the interactivity relevant to your market sector. Some good examples include the Automobile Association (AA) that offers a members service, where customers e-mail their travel departure and arrival destinations and the AA in return forwards a route map to them. This kind of creative and customized interaction will lead, of course, to substantial customer satisfaction, but you have to be able to deliver what you promise within the timescale you set out.

Other examples of creative interactivity can be found at the Halifax site (http://www.halifax.co.uk) where the bank provides its online visitors with a mortgage calculator. Another creative interactive feature is evident at the woman's 'lifestyle' e-zine, BeMe.com (see Figure 5.6). Users scan in personal pictures of themselves and change hair colour, haircuts and lip shade onscreen before they make that all-important visit to the hairdresser or beauty salon. The Guinness Site (http://www. guiness.com), however, offers one of the more humorous instances of creative interactivity. It has a 'Boss Panic Button' on its site which

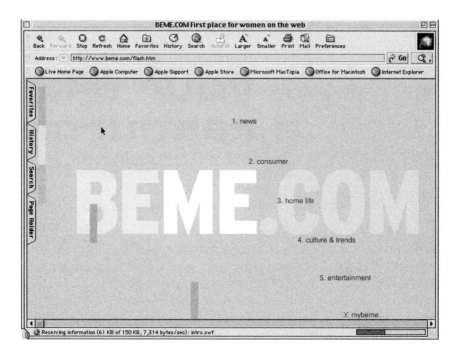

Figure 5.6 BeMe.com encourages interactivity

links to a boring-looking spreadsheet, in the event of any unwelcome prying eyes.

Summary

Making your site interactive can serve to create loyalty by getting audiences involved in an online community; it can keep people longer at your site by satisfying itchy fingers, and can ultimately make people feel closer to your business. Having a static Web site that resembles a brochure full of glib ad-speak is therefore no longer enough; to stay ahead of the online business revolution you will need to approach the Internet on its own, interactive terms.

six

Make **your site a resource**

Any member of your target audience using the Internet to find information about your business is likely to make your Web site their first port of call. Having a business presence on the Web is no longer sufficient, it is now the type of presence you have which matters. This chapter will help you think about how your Web site can effectively communicate your business identity by turning it into a resource providing relevant information to your target audiences.

Whatever you may like to think, the main reason people go online is to acquire information, not to spend money. It sounds obvious, but the best way to capitalize on the information age is by providing information (and in some cases lots of it). No matter how much information you provide on your site, keep navigation as simple as possible and provide a search engine if your site warrants it.

The information product

The businesses that succeed on the Internet do so by appreciating the fact that it is, above all else, an information resource. E-businesses therefore need to move beyond the mentality that a Web site is purely and simply about selling products. Sure, people do and will spend on the Internet, but this isn't usually their initial intention. They want solutions to problems and answers to questions. They want, in other words, information.

As well as displaying their wares, e-businesses also need to become 'information suppliers', building relations with their public by satisfying their Internet needs. Your Web site needs to supply relevant information in order to add value to your visitor's online experience.

By delivering the 'information product' you will be able to establish strong relations with your different and diverse audiences.

Site close-up

Blackstar – http://www.blackstar.co.uk

Online video and DVD retailer Blackstar provides visitors with a very user-friendly and informative online experience. The site is a model of easy navigation with an incredibly straightforward search facility. All product listings include a brief synopsis along with relevant technical information, which helps visitors decide whether they are buying the right thing. Blackstar's site is the very essence of what constitutes a good e-PR site by using information as a form of persuasion (see Figure 6.1).The sort of information you should have on your site includes:

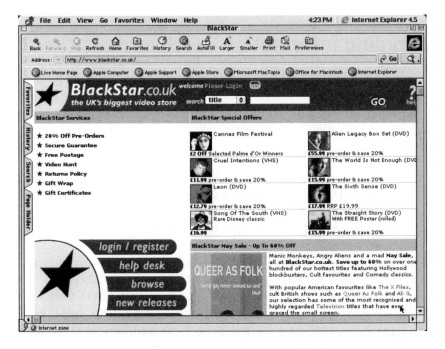

Figure 6.1 Blackstar's site is the very essence of what constitutes a good e-PR site

- Product information. Be as interactive as possible by providing questions relating to your customers' requirements and then leading them to the most suitable product.
- Company information of relevance to your audience.
- Informative feature articles. Don't follow the bad example of some companies that lift articles from trade publications as copyright laws still apply on the Net. Write your own instead.
- Interviews with authoritative or well-known figures within your industry.
- Question and answer pages.
- Informative events, such as online seminars and conferences.
- Press releases and other media-friendly information.
- Advice columns. Offer advice and 'how to' tips relating to your market or audience. L'Oreal's Web site (http://www. loreal.com), for instance, offers health and beauty tips on make-up and skin tones – this works because it is relevant both to the company and to the audience. Try and think of advice you could offer that is relevant to your business. If you sell organic food products, you should provide lots of healthy recipes using natural ingredients.

Avoiding information overload

While useful information is essential on your site, it must be visually accessible. Solid, unbroken text on the Net tends to put people off. To overcome the negative effects of 'information overload' you need to make your information Net-friendly. You should:

- Minimize information on your home page. Don't burden visitors with information that may not be relevant to them the moment they enter.
- Break up text into digestible chunks. Place gaps between paragraphs.
- Use a clear font. Linguistic researchers have discovered that Verdona and Arial fonts are the easiest to read quickly.
- Write clearly. Just because you understand what you have written does not mean that your audience will understand it. Therefore, write in a style that all your audience understands. Avoid 'official' and 'academic' language.

- Keep backgrounds simple. When you have more than one paragraph on a page, keep backgrounds simple by using a solid block of colour.
- Use different font sizes to liven up text. Make headings, subheadings, keywords and phrases a different (bigger) size to the standard text.
- Make sure your site is easy to navigate. No page should be more than three clicks away from another.
- Make links obvious. 'Press releases' is a better name for a link to a press release archive than, say, 'Media Source'.

Develop your site so visitors return regularly to find out information about your products, services and industry. One way of doing this is by adding calendars that have your company's key dates on them (http://www.freescript.com can direct you to calendar programs). A lot of servers, including Lotus, Netscape, Microsoft and Novell, already offer calendars in their packages.

A private area at your Web site should have your diary, appointments and meetings on (a password would have to be set up to enter this area). Authorized users can find out what is happening and where – which would result in users having closer ties with your company.

Another way of becoming an information resource is by becoming a broadcast site. Users can ask to be sent new information on a relevant subject as soon as it is published. Broadcast systems include BlackWeb (http://www.blackWeb.com) and Marimba (http://www. marimba.com).

Syndication

If you feel you do not have enough interesting information on your site, or if you find it hard to update this information constantly, syndication is the solution. Syndication refers to information you can put on your Web site, which comes direct from online news feeds. Syndicated content can be a very effective way of building relations with your visitors, providing them with relevant and regularly updated information.

'Aggregator' sites such as Moreover (http://www.moreover.com) or iSyndicate (http://www.isyndicate.com) collect new stories from a cross-section of sources and convert them into HTML code. By registering with them (for free), you can customize news information by adding a news feed to your site. Both sites provide a three-step process to putting a syndication facility on your site:

- First, you select the type of feed you want (there are hundreds to choose from).
- Second, you decide the layout you want. You can specify the column width, font style and colour scheme you require.
- Finally, you add the relevant news feed to your site by copying and pasting a chunk of HTML script.

The news feeds you can choose from cover specific areas such as international news, domestic news, business, sport, arts and media as well as providing a general news option.

The promise of continually updated information makes using syndication an effective way of keeping site–visitor relations alive by making your site more 'sticky'.

Audience agenda

In the second chapter of this book I stressed the importance of setting objectives. Indeed, objectives are essential as they provide you with focus and a direction in which your e-PR efforts will head. Your objectives, however, should not get in the way of the objectives of your audience.

The paradox of Internet marketing, therefore, is that to meet your e-business agenda you need to abandon it. You may set yourself the objective to increase online sales of a product by 100 per cent but this is not going to help you decide what to put on your Web site. After all, the only true measurement of a site's success that counts is the degree to which it meets the agenda of its visitors.

Instead, you need to entice your Web visitors with what they require, then integrate this with what you want. There are four real reasons why people decide to go on the Web. In descending order, these are:

- To get information. As I have mentioned before, people decide to go online to find answers to questions and solutions to problems.

- To interact. The Internet is an interactive medium. It's just a pity that Web visitors seem to understand this better than Web developers.
- To get stuff. This is where your objectives overlap with those of your audience.
- To be entertained. The Web is a media channel and just like other media channels it is used for the purpose of entertainment.

If your site can satisfy your audience's hunger for information, interaction, products and entertainment, you will have a clear head start. The answer to why your business launched into cyberspace should never be 'Because it's there'. A Web site takes time and careful consideration. Furthermore, to be a success it must stem from your audience's agenda, not your own.

Site close-up

FT.com – (http://www.ft.com)

The online version of the *Financial Times* has fast become one of the most talked about new sites on the Web. The site has even received masses of publicity offline (and not just in the *Financial Times*). The main reason for this is the wealth of information the FT is willing to give away free. Its Archive area is an incredible resource, with over six million archives from 3,000 publications, background information on over 20,000 companies and a set of dossiers on key business people. The site also features discussion forums, career advice and a handy virtual office with e-mail, file storage and online diary capabilities (see Figure 6.2).

Update your site

Long-term site–visitor relations depend on repeat traffic. Your site needs to keep clients and customers coming back even when they don't want to buy something from you, so when they do they will automatically think of your site. People are unlikely to return to your site unless you update it and (perhaps more importantly) make sure people realize that it is regularly updated. If visitors pay two or three repeat visits and find it has not been updated they will stop coming back.

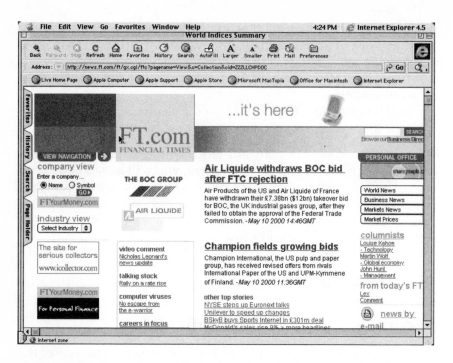

Figure 6.2 *The Financial Times'* site features discussion forums, career advice and a handy virtual office with e-mail, file storage and online diary capabilities

When you are planning your Web site decide which pages you are going to update, and how often. If you have the time and resources it is a good idea to update some small sections daily (such as a 'Tip of the Day' or something similar), a page you update weekly (for instance, 'This Week's Market News') and a larger section you update monthly.

You should never let information pass its sell-by date as this will send out a wrong signal. If you do not have the time to update your site more than once a month, you must at least make sure the information on your site is still relevant. A page called 'February Events' is no use to people visiting the site in April!

Third-party endorsement

For information to be well received, it needs to be endorsed. In the 'real world', PR people claim that PR is more effective than advertising because it depends on third-party endorsement. PR messages are received via an intermediary, such as a journalist, and are therefore considered less biased and more believable than advertising.

With a Web site, however, your business does not communicate **via** the media because it is a part **of** the media. Your Web site is more likely to be considered a useful resource by your visitors if they are shown that other people feel the same way. Therefore, the challenge businesses face on the Web is that, if they want to make their site act as an effective PR vehicle, they need to add an element of third-party endorsement that isn't there to begin with. Here are some ways in which you can add authority to your site via third-party endorsement:

- **Celebrity endorsement.** The one sure-fire way to generate interest in your site is to get a celebrity onboard. Try and think of which celebrities would be relevant to your target audience. Then put a proposal together stating what exactly the particular celebrity would get out of such endorsement and send it to the agent via post or e-mail. A list of celebrity agencies is available on Yell (http://www.yell.co.uk) as well as in other online telephone directories. Marks and Spencer is one company that uses celebrities appropriate to their products and the audience on their site. They currently have a picture of celebrity fitness guru Rosemary Conely with a hand-written message underneath inviting us to enjoy one of her healthy choice recipes.
- **Quote from the press.** If you have received positive press coverage, incorporate quotes from favourable features in your site. Many companies, such as World Pop (http://www. worldpop.com), devote an entire page for this purpose.
- **Include client or customer testimonials on your site.** If you have happy customers who are willing to endorse your site, contact them via e-mail and ask for a quote.
- **Employee endorsement.** An employee isn't, strictly speaking, a third party, but as employees are an important audience, employee endorsement can be effective. For instance, the supermarket chain Asda (http://www.asda.com) uses a different in-store personality each week to help visitors around the site ('Hello, I'm Phil Hayes. Let me show you some of the new products you can find in store this week'). This form of endorsement has a positive effect on both the internal audience (by making

employees feel involved in the e-PR process) and external audiences (by giving a personal face to the company). Employee endorsement is particularly useful for large companies and organizations.

- **Mention awards.** Mention any awards or industry recognition received by your business or site.
- **Add a discussion group or bulletin board.** Adding a discussion group or bulletin board to your site will only create a sense of third-party endorsement if visitors are saying positive things! Providing you monitor these forums effectively, however, they can be extremely powerful e-PR tools (see the next chapter).
- **Case studies.** Case studies add weight to your site–visitor relations. Case studies on consumer sites tend to work best when they are about individuals. People like reading about people; it's as simple as that. Visitors like to read about situations that relate to them. They like, for instance, to know that a problem they have had isn't unique. If possible, you could include testimonials from satisfied customers too. Many business-to-business companies provide a list of companies they have worked for with links to their site. This is a mistake and will only lead people away from your site. Instead you should link to case studies of how you helped each company. Starfish Communications (http://www.starfish.co.uk) and my own site, Peppermint PR (http://www.peppermintpr.co.uk) are two examples of businesses that use the case study to great effect.

Become a third party

If you don't want to depend on third-party endorsement you can always turn your site itself into a third party. This involves devoting at least part of your site to something not directly related to your product or service, but relevant to your audience.

This can help you more directly meet the needs of your audience and will benefit your product and service by the power of association. By becoming a third party, you will also be adding authority to your site by rendering it more objective. More and more successful e-businesses are using this technique to great e-PR effect. Absolut Vodka (http://www.absolutvodka.com), for instance, devotes its entire site to 'club and DJ culture', to appeal to the youth market they target. The Absolut product benefits by being associated with the lifestyle interests of its audience. It also serves to associate the product with a context (night clubs) where it is likely to be consumed.

Summary

To engage in successful relationships with your customers you need to appreciate their expectations by becoming an information provider. You have to move away from thinking your Web site is only about advertising and selling your products or services. To add value to your audience's online experience you need to deliver knowledge in a usable and imaginative way. The secret to making your site an effective e-PR tool is to exploit two of the Internet's defining features, interaction and information.

seven

Search **engines**

Search engines and other directories are in many ways the most significant of all online media as they provide the most populated route towards a Web site. Some surveys claim that over 80 per cent of people wanting to find information online use a search engine to help them. It is certainly true that search engines help most Internet users find material relevant to them. Of an estimated 500 million Web pages to choose from, even the most comprehensive search engines only cover between 10–20 per cent of them. Yet the fact is that more than half of all site visits originate from search engines.

To make sure your site reaches the audiences you want it to you need to be part of that 10–20 per cent; you must therefore register with all the major search engines.

The hardest audience

Search engines and directories are not only a means of reaching your audience as they constitute an important and discriminating audience in themselves. While submitting a site to the main search engines is essential, success is by no means guaranteed as the human and non-human members of the search engine audience may be the hardest of all to win over.

However, by considering the search engines as an audience in their own right, rather than merely a means of reaching your audiences, you will already have given yourself a head start.

Before you register

Before discussing what you should do when you visit a search engine, we should look at what happens when a search engine visits you. This can happen either before or after you register with a search site. Search engines exist to provide a worthwhile service to people searching at their sites. It therefore doesn't matter how many tricks you use to get your site ranked in a preferential position; if your site is not up to scratch you have little chance of being indexed.

Although some of the main search engines depend on automatic 'robots' to index sites, their sophisticated nature means that even without the aid of human discretion they will be able to judge the quality of your site. Before you submit your site to the search engines, you have to make sure that it will make the grade. To make your site search engine friendly, you will need to do the following:

- Update your site. Search engines know that people are more likely to visit and return to sites that are regularly updated.
- Obtain your own domain. If you have your own domain name it will be a lot easier to make an impact on the major search engines, especially Yahoo! Having your own domain name communicates your commitment to your site in a way that having a site hosted by your ISP (Internet Service Provider) does not. Domain name registration provides one easy way search engines can discriminate among the plethora of sites submitted to them. http://www.mysite.com would therefore be given preference over http://www.demon.net/mysite.
- Make sure your links work. Links that lead to an out-of-date URL can easily be checked by search engines, so be careful.
- Make sure your site is compatible with most browsers – checking your site from different browsers will help you make sure it looks good to visitors and search engines alike.

The next step

Once you are fully satisfied with the form and function of your site, there is one more step you need to take before submitting it to search engines. When evaluating your site, search engines not only rely on the descriptions you provide them with at their site. They also categorize sites based on 'META tag' descriptions embedded within your HTML code. These descriptions are 'read' by automatic 'robots' that analyse every transmitted site. Therefore, the key to being picked up by search engines is often locked within the 'hyper-text' of your site.

Spiders and crawlers

These are not the names of forthcoming X-rated movies, but 'robot' programs used by search engines that visit your site, index your content, and then list it on the engine. Although they are not human and lack the power of sophisticated thought, they can and do discriminate between Web sites. These non-human visitors must therefore be regarded as audiences that need to be impressed.

You can influence robots, spiders and crawlers by incorporating keywords and descriptions into the HTML code used to build and design Web sites. Furthermore, if you have a page of your site that you want to avoid being indexed on a search engine because it changes all the time, you can tell the 'autobots' this in your site's META tags.

META tags

META tags are HTML instructions that contain your keywords and help search engine 'autobots' index your site. Without META tags, every single word on your site will be treated as a keyword. All the main search engines rely, in part, on the META tag to categorize your site effectively.

To view your site's META tags, go into your site and click on 'Source' then 'View'; the HTML text (including the META tags) will then appear on the screen. A good tip is to use this process to look at the META tags of Web sites that appear high on search engines to get an idea of the sort of keywords and descriptions that work.

It is perfectly possible to build a site and ignore these META tags as they do not alter or affect what the visitor sees. However, if you are concerned about being included on search engines (and you should be) you need to treat META tags with the respect that they deserve.

The main META tags

Whether you use a Web site design agency, a Web-building software package (such as Dreamweaver) or construct your site's code yourself using HTML, you need to be aware of the main types of META tags. Not all META tags are equal, and some have no e-PR signifi-cance whatsoever. The main ones you need to know about are description and keyword tags, although the 'robots' tag may also prove useful. Each tag is incorporated within the HEAD section at the start of each page's HTML text. The format is as follows:

Your Web page
<META name = 'description' content = 'A description of your Web page or site should be included here'>
<META name = 'keywords' content = 'list. Keywords here'>

The 'description' META tag

META descriptions should be between 15 and 30 words in length, and give a general flavour of what visitors can expect from your site or page without burdening them with too much information. The description tag can be based on the description you submit to the search engine directly.

The 'keywords' META tag

The 'keywords' META tag provides you with the opportunity to enter a list of relevant keywords for your site. Think of the audi-ences you are trying to attract when forming the list of your key-words – avoid professional terms, for instance, if your main target is a consumer audience.

The 'robots' META tag

If you want a search engine to ignore a specific page due to its con-stantly changing nature, put the following command in the HEAD section of the relevant page(s):

<META name = 'robots' CONTENT = 'No index, no follow'>

The 'title' tag

The 'title' tag is not called a META tag, although it functions in a similar way. Search engines read the HTML 'title' and display that information on their searches. Furthermore, search engines value the words in the title tag as more significant than any other words in your HTML text excluding META tags. In fact, some search engines (of which AltaVista is one) can narrow searches down to an index of page titles.

The rules for title tags are as follows:

- Make sure every page has a title tag. Unlike META tags, title tags are visible to your visitors and so omitting a title tag is a faux pas that will get noticed.
- Keep titles short. I would recommend a maximum of seven words.
- Make titles descriptive. There are two reasons for this. The first is that descriptive titles will help move search engines traffic towards your site. The second is that, however long a page takes to load, the title loads almost instantaneously. Visitors with more lethargic Web connections can therefore get an indication of whether your site is for them before the page appears.

Tag aid

If the idea of being solely responsible for your HTML and META tags is a bit too much to take, there is help out there. META tag services and advice can be found at the following URL's:

Web site Promote http://www.Web sitepromote.com

Northern Webs http://www.northernWebs.com/set/setsimjr.html

Site Up http://www.siteup.com/meta.html

Yahoo! http://www.yahoo.com/Computers_and_Internet/ Information_and_Documentation/Data_Formats/HTML/META_ Tag/

How to register with search engines

There are two ways you can get your site listed with the main search engines:

1. You can use an automated program, such as Submit It! (http://www.submitit.com), that will register automatically with over 100 search engines (see Figure 7.1).

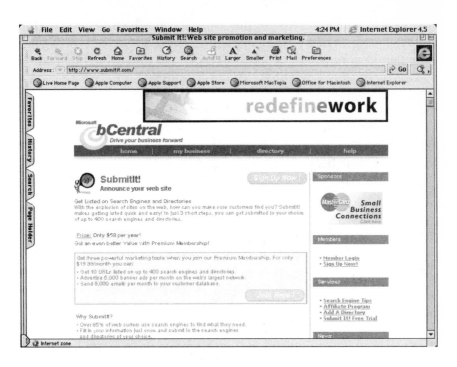

Figure 7.1 Submit It! is an automated search engine

2. You can visit each search engine individually and manually fill out an electronic registration form on each one.

While number one may look like the most attractive option, it may not be the most successful. If you use an automated program, you will only be asked for two descriptions of your site (one short, one long). This means you cannot tailor the information to each individual search engine and each audience using each search engine.

If you want to combine successful e-PR with effective time management, my advice is to register individually with five of the big search engines then use Submit It! for the rest.

Keywords and descriptions

Each search engine requires you to submit keywords and descriptions of varying lengths relating to your site. Generally, you are required to provide a longer description than the one you used in the META tag. When writing keywords, think about the words your target audiences would be likely to type in to find a site like yours.

Tips on writing keywords and descriptions:

- Think like your audience and base keywords on benefits – value, relaxation, adventure and so on.
- Include the names of your competitors so when people look for competitors they will find you alongside them.
- Include your company name and each product or service you provide.
- Use your top ten keywords as the basis of your description.

Yahoo!

Submission Page: http://www.yahoo.com/info/suggest/

Yahoo!, the biggest and most popular search engine/directory of them all, is the most important place for your site to get listed (see Figure 7.2).

Although the term search engine implies a mechanical process, the Yahoo! submission process is very subjective and based on human interaction. Yahoo! has a staff of hundreds who assess each submission and decide whether it should be included in the directory. This means that, as well as a means of reaching your audiences, Yahoo! should be regarded as an audience itself.

Here is the Yahoo! registration process:

- Go to the submission page.
- Write the name of your company and Web address.
- Find the category you want your site to be listed under.
- Add keywords that are comparable to index headings or topics. For instance, if you sell mountain climbing equipment you could list words such as mountain, climbing, sports, outdoors, travel, exercise, hiking, abseiling, etc. Each engine requires a different number of keywords (5–10).
- Provide a 20-word description of what your company does.
- For Yahoo!, select the category you want to be listed in, eg Business_and_Commerce: Public Relations Agencies.
- List your name and e-mail address.

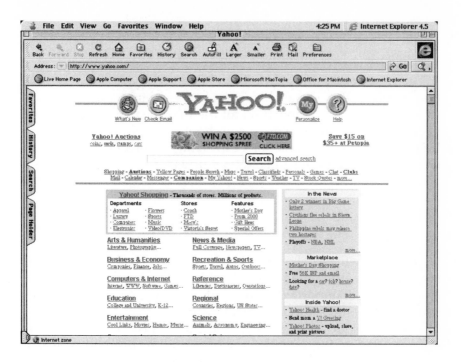

Figure 7.2 Yahoo! is the biggest search engine of them all

- Click on the 'submit' button.
- You will receive confirmation by e-mail.
- List your registration into additional categories. This is especially beneficial if you sell multiple products.

Other major search engines include:

- **AltaVista.** Submission page:
  http://www.altavista.com/av/content/addurl.htm
- **Excite.** Submission page: http://www.excite.com/info/add-url/
- **HotBot.** Submission page:
  http://www.hotbot.com/addurl.asp
- **Lycos.** Submission page:
  http://www.lycos.com/addasite.html

For a comprehensive list of search engines, visit The Web Site Top 100: http://www.mmgco/top100.html

Evaluate your success

To see how successful your efforts have been, you can use a free online tool called Rank This (http://www.rankthis.com) to see where the site is positioned on all the main search engines when people type in your keywords. You should monitor your ranking at least once a month as positions can change at breakneck speed, as new sites are submitted and old ones updated.

Summary

Registering with search engines is not an e-PR option, it is an e-PR essential. The humans and 'robots' behind the search engines form one of the most important online audiences of all. Submitting your site to search engines and preparing your META text for visits from their robots is the first e-PR step you should take once your site is up and running. It is only the first of many, however; while search engines help you start relations they are not much good at building them. To do this properly, you need to look beyond search engines into other forms of what we shall call 'active e-PR'.

eight

Action e-PR

A great deal of e-PR depends on an element of chance. For instance, you can use every technique possible to get your site a good search engine ranking and still fail. This doesn't mean you shouldn't do it; search engine registration is an integral e-PR activity. What it does mean, however, is that you should look at other online methods of promoting your site that you have more control over. This chapter looks at 'action e-PR' techniques, which enable you to influence your audience by directing them to your site. These techniques include actions you can take, as well as actions your visitors can be encouraged to take.

Action e-PR refers to the ways in which you can take positive action beyond your site to increase the numbers of relevant visitors to your site. Although registering your site with the main search engines could be viewed as action e-PR, the term more specifically refers to those activities that eliminate the elements of chance. Examples of such activities are detailed in this chapter.

Announcement services

Due to the ever-increasing amount of new sites that are launched into cyberspace every single day, there are now services solely devoted to announcing new sites. These services help people interested in the Internet keep up-to-date with the latest online developments. Announcement sites typically allow you to submit your URL along with a description of what visitors are able to find at your site. When writing descriptions of your site you should:

- **Identify your audience**. Announcement pages are read by people with a diverse range of interests. Unlike search engines, visitors are not always able to conduct keyword searches.

Therefore, make sure you identify exactly whom your site will appeal to.

- **Be clear**. List the things people will be able to do and find at your site. You can use the site description you submitted to search engines to help you do this.
- **Be correct**. Check your spelling and grammar before you submit your description as you only get one chance.

The useful thing with announcement services is that they usually allow you to announce your site more than once, so every time you update it you can submit a new site description. Among the most popular announcement services there are Netscape's 'What's New' page (see Figure 8.1):
(http://www.netscape.com/netcenter/new.html)
and UK Yell's announcement page:
(http://www.Yell.co.uk/ukyw/whats_new/index.html)

Figure 8.1 Netscape is one of the big Internet firms that offer announcement services

Relevant links

Links are a great way of reaching a broader section of your target market. The benefits of getting reciprocal links with other sites are manifold. Here are some of them:

- increase in traffic to your site;
- improved competitor and trade relations;
- heightened interactivity on your site (if you include reciprocal links).

However, not all links are equal. Some people play the numbers game, believing that the more links they have to their site the better, regardless of where they come from. Viewing things from an e-PR perspective, you will understand that this is the wrong approach. It is not the amount of traffic to your site that is important, but the relevance of that traffic to your online interests. There is no point, for example, negotiating a link from a feng shui consultant if you run an online car auction site. Obviously, the links your site requires are those from relevant or related sites. These sites do not have to be direct competitors; they just need to attract a similar target audience. For instance, an upmarket online wine merchant may benefit by having a link from a reputable cheese delicatessen site.

When you conducted competitor research online, you will have come across a plethora of sites relevant to your own. These are a good place to start in your hunt for reciprocal links. When searching for new sites you should follow these steps in order to get links to your site:

- Use the search engines to help find sites related to yours (competitors, trade organizations, e-zines, etc).
- Visit the sites that come up and see if they contain links to similar sites.
- If they do, send an e-mail message to the contact or site owner.
- Tell the contact you think their site (which you should name) is great, and explain why.
- Ask the contact if they would consider linking to your site. Give them a good reason (don't feel obliged to offer a reciprocal link unless it would be appropriate).
- Provide a short and succinct description of your site.
- Thank the contact in advance, whatever their decision.

Finding appropriate sites and asking for links should be a continuous and ongoing part of the e-PR activity. Try to contact at least 10 new sites a month. After a while, you will find that other sites will link to yours without your having to ask, and the amount of relevant traffic arriving at your site will increase at a significant rate.

There are many so-called 'Free-For-All' (FFA) link sites out there that will only serve to throw you off the scent in your e-PR quest for relevant links. The apparent advantage of these services is that they provide link lists that anyone can add to without paying for the privilege. This 'advantage', however, is also a problem: *anyone* can add to a link list. That means a lot of sites that fail to make the grade with the search engines turn to the FFA sites as a last resort. As these sites encourage reciprocal links, the consequence of this FFA approach could result in an e-PR disaster. You could be linked with shady e-business sites, explicit erotica sites, and even 'My Pet Dog' type home pages. This will hardly make the right impression with your target audiences and will increase the amount of irrelevant e-mail.

Web rings

Web rings are online 'linked communities' of Web sites centred on one topic. The way they work is that every site participating in the ring will link to the previous and next site participating in the ring (but not every other site in the ring), as well as to the main page that gives a full list of all the sites within the ring. They are called 'rings' because, in theory at least, all the participating sites are linked together in a 'cyber circle', so by clicking continuously on the 'Next' option, users should be able to boomerang around the ring, returning to the site where they started.

The largest Web ring organizer on the Internet is the suitably titled Webring (http://www.Webring.org). Webring coordinates over 60,000 rings with over half a million sites participating. It enables you to join a new ring, see what rings are available and even start your own Web ring. The size of each ring varies greatly. There are rings of five sites and others of five hundred sites.

The advantages of participating in a Web ring are clear:

- It will increase the number of new visitors arriving at your site.
- Every one of these visitors will be interested in your site's subject.

░ It will improve your competitor relations by connecting you to the sites of potential competitors in an online community working on the principle of mutual benefit.

Before deciding whether it would be appropriate for your site to participate in a Web ring, visit the Web ring site and search its database to see if there are any sites that suit your site. If there are not, you may even consider starting your own Web ring.

If you are interested in the idea of a Web ring, you could also look at Sadiq's Webring Directory (http://www.users.dircon.co.uk/-majaffer/Webrings1), which is stacked full of useful information on the subject.

Bookmarks

A bookmark is a software tool that enables people to store URLs (Web site addresses) they want to visit. Both Netscape Navigator and Internet Explorer offer their users a variety of bookmark tools. One direct way of generating repeat traffic is therefore to offer a friendly reminder to bookmark your site by placing a notice on each page saying 'Bookmark this site!'

Browsers also let their users know when a particular bookmarked site has been updated. Netscape Navigator, for instance, contacts the Web servers that store the pages, checks the dates when the Web pages were last changed and compares those dates to the dates when you last viewed the pages. It then displays a window that tells the user how many of the Web pages it succeeded in checking and how many of them have changed. An unchanged page is indicated with a solid green bookmark icon and a changed page has two grey bars on its icon. You can guarantee that people are more likely to return to sites with grey bars than those with green bookmark icons.

Starting pages

If you use Netscape Navigator or Internet Explorer, it is quite likely that their home page appears on your screen when you log on. However, both browsers enable users to use any other sites for starting pages. If people used your page as their starting page they would be reminded of your site every time they went online. Post a message on your home page asking people to change their starting page to yours, and offer them a reason why they should want to (if you are an e-commerce site you could offer daily discount coupons, if you are in the service sector you could use your useful 'tips of the day' as an incentive).

As people may not automatically know how to replace their start page, you should make sure that lack of knowledge would not prevent them by providing the following guidelines:

- You can choose a new start page for your browser from the Internet Options box.
- To access the Internet Options box select 'View' then 'Internet Options'.
- Type the address (or URL) of the new home page into the Internet Options box.

By providing your site visitors with these instructions, you will benefit in two ways. It will increase the chance of visitors making your page their starting page as well as help to make your site a resource of valuable and objective information.

History list

A history list is a record of visited Web pages on your visitor's browser. It helps people visit sites they have forgotten to bookmark. To access the list they select 'Tools' then 'History', and then all they have to do is click on the item they want in the history.

Many regular Internet users use history lists as a way of saving online Net-surfing time to visit sites they clearly already know have proved useful to them before. Users can search the list by defining conditions such as 'Visit count is greater than 3'. This command would bring up only those sites they have visited more than three times. The different conditions relate to visit frequency, site size, as well as when the page was first and last visited.

To make sure your site continually comes up in the history list searches you therefore need to make sure you generate repeat traffic, as well as having lots of different Web pages.

Mailing list updates

One more direct way of encouraging repeat visits is to create a personalized mailing list and then send site update notices to subscribers. Even if you are ranked high on history lists and visitors have bookmarked your site, you still cannot guarantee repeat traffic due to the amount of choices your audience faces in cyberspace. For this reason you may decide to be a little more proactive in your e-PR efforts by asking people to join your mailing list. You can then send the visitors who have expressed an interest in your site e-mail messages every time you update your site, with a hypertext link to your home page.

If you are doing this, you need to make clear on your subscription form that subscribers will receive update notices. In addition, you must take care not to send them e-mails every single day. If your site *is* updated on a daily basis, wait until it has a significant addition or alteration before sending out your update messages. So, if you have an online newsletter, it is better to incorporate site update notices into the newsletter than send out separate e-mails to people who have subscribed because they wanted newsletters not updates.

'Favorite' menus

The Favorites menu is available to users of Internet Explorer and Netscape Navigator as a place in which to store URLs they want to revisit. It provides a similar function to the bookmark facility, and enables users to return to a marked Web site with a single click. It can therefore provide people with another valuable short cut to your site. Many people, however, don't know how Favorite menus work and often don't know they exist. It may prove worthwhile to offer a helping hand at your site, so that your site will automatically become your visitor's first Favorite. You will need to provide the following instructions:

1. Favorite menus are accessed through Windows and Office programs.
2. The command sequence is 'Start' – 'Favorites'.
3. To add a Web page to the menu, select 'Add to Favorites'.

4. Enter the Web site address in the dialogue box.
5. To put the new Favorite into a sub-folder of the main folder, click the 'Create In' button and pick the sub-folder into which you want to put the new Favorite.
6. To make a new folder for the Favorite, select a folder in which to put the new folder and then click on 'New Folder'.

Summary

Although registering with search engines is an integral part of your e-PR activity, there are other e-PR actions you can take which eliminate the element of 'pot luck' inherent in search engine site registration. These actions include announcing your site with an announcement service, negotiating relevant links to your site and getting visitors to use bookmark tools to your advantage.

nine

E-mail **essentials**

Despite the hype that surrounds the World Wide Web, e-mail remains the most universally used application on the Internet. It is also one of the most important e-PR tools of all.

Public relations is about communication and the way people communicate with one another online is via e-mail. Whether you are contributing to a newsgroup, answering a customer enquiry, providing information to journalists or holding an online seminar, the application you use is e-mail. E-mail can help you get to know your publics, and allows your publics to get to know you.

To conduct effective e-PR you therefore need to understand how e-mail can be used to the greatest effect. The purpose of this chapter is to move towards such understanding and to provide an awareness of the e-mail essentials that will assist your e-PR efforts. We will explore both why and how you should use e-mail, starting with the types of e-mail applications out there.

Applications

To receive and respond to e-mail messages you need e-mail software that works in conjunction with your Internet Service Provider (ISP). The e-mail application you use most probably came free with your ISP – Microsoft's Outlook Express and Netscape Communicator are the most widely used applications.

While these applications perform their functions perfectly well, from an e-PR perspective they are not necessarily the best. If you want to take your e-PR efforts seriously you could look at some other packages such as Eudora Pro (http://www.eudora.com) that allow you automatically to prioritize e-mail messages and have an automatic spell-check. Eudora Pro also has a powerful e-mail filter system. Other e-mail programs suitable for e-PR purposes include:

- **Microsoft Outlook.** – http://www.microsoft.com/outlook
- **The Bat.** – http://www.ritlabs.com/the_bat/
- **DTS Mail.** – http://dtsoftware.simplenet.com/
- **Power Mail (Macintosh).** – http://www.ctmdev.com/

All these applications provide folders features. These work like the folders under Windows, enabling you to arrange incoming messages by storing them in different folders. Before deciding which application is right for you, try a few out, and work out which features you prefer.

The role of e-mail in e-PR

You can use e-mail to communicate with all your key audiences (employees, customers, investors and journalists) as it can be used to:

- respond to customer enquiries;
- distribute information within your company;
- send newsletters to subscribers;
- contribute to discussion groups;
- contact journalists.

However, despite the efficient and flexible nature of e-mail, it must be used correctly by everyone in your company. Unfortunately, many companies fail to realize that there are right and wrong ways to use e-mail and that getting an e-mail message right is as important as getting a standard press release or business letter right. One misjudged e-mail message can do untold damage to your business. E-mail is a powerful tool, and as such it must be used with great care.

The main reason why people go online is still to look at and respond to e-mail messages. Furthermore, the significance of e-mail is increasing as technological advancements in mobile communications and WAP technology mean you can access e-mails from just about anywhere.

E-mail efficiency

E-mail is in many ways the most convenient communication tool of all, either on or offline. These are the main benefits of this modern marvel:

- **Cost.** E-mail enables you to send messages around the world at local telephone rates.
- **Speed.** It takes only a few seconds to send a message from New York to New South Wales.
- **Availability.** E-mail is an insomniac communications tool, available 24 hours a day, 365 days a year.
- **Convenience**. E-mail allows you to send as many messages to as many people as you want to, whenever and wherever. The nature of e-mail is such that people respond to questions at exactly the time they want to.
- **Environmental.** The only resource e-mail uses is electricity.

All of these benefits, coupled with the rise of the Internet itself, mean that it is fast becoming *the* way to communicate with target audiences.

Automatic response

In an ideal world, every e-mail message you receive would be responded to individually. In reality, of course, this isn't always possible – as you could be receiving hundreds of e-mails a day. If people are requiring the same information, set up a file library of responses to FAQs and respond to each similar message with a cut-and-pasted prepared response.

Even this process can become too time-consuming after a while, however, so you may need to consider using an automatic response software program from your ISP. To use these programs effectively you need to set up different mailboxes for different types of messages such as:

latestnews@mycompany.com
or
newproduct@mycompany.com

The automatic response software automatically responds to a message with information relating to the latest company news or a new product depending on the mailbox the original message was sent to. Although this solution is not ideal, it is a way of keeping relationships alive when you do not have the time to respond to e-mails yourself.

As simple as a Bcc:

The key to successful relationships is to make people feel important. If you have one message to send to one hundred people, you do not want to advertise the fact by listing each individual e-mail address. At the same time, you don't want to have to post the message one hundred times over. This is where the Bcc: (Blind Carbon Copy) function comes in handy. Instead of typing all the addresses in the Cc: (Carbon Copy) box, you can make these addresses invisible to the eyes of each recipient by using the Bcc: box. This way you can send an apparently individual message to an entire target audience simultaneously.

Emoticons

The drawback with e-mail communication is that the tone and emotion that can be expressed via telecommunication are lost. To make the tone of a message more obvious online some people use icons that indicate emotion, 'emoticons', by resembling a face on its side. The most common symbols people use are these (tilt your head to the left to see each face):

: –) a happy face	; –) a wink
: – (an unhappy face	: – I an angry face
: – / a confused face	: – o a shocked face
8 –) cool! (a face with sunglasses)	

There are, however, two problems with 'emoticons'. The first is that many people do not understand what they mean and just think they are errors in the text. The second is that, among those who do understand them, many people find them annoying and tacky. My view is that, while 'emoticons' may be acceptable in informal messages, using them in your business communications will not aid your e-PR efforts. I have listed them here so you will be able to understand them when they are incorporated in messages you receive.

Subject lines

The strength of your subject line determines whether your e-mail address will be read. Here are some basic points to think about when writing a subject line:

- **Be brief.** A subject line should ideally be no longer than eight words.
- Avoid over-emphasis. CAPITAL LETTERS AND EXCLAMATION MARKS LOOK LIKE YOU ARE TRYING TOO HARD!!! As with all e-PR, subtlety is the key to success.
- **Be specific.** When replying to someone's e-mail, use his or her subject line with whatever extra information is needed.
- **Be informal.** Successful online business communications depend on the personal touch.
- **Be honest.** If you are sending a commercial e-mail or press release, don't use generic subject lines such as 'Your phone call'.
- **Be correct.** Poor spelling anywhere in an e-mail sends the wrong signals.
- **Be a tease.** Hint at your message content without giving people the whole picture.

The body of your e-mail

Having managed to get people to read your message, you now need to make sure you get it right. So here are the golden rules of writing effective messages:

- **Put it in context.** If you are responding to a message, make sure you put your reply in context by quoting from their e-mail.
- **Spell-check.** Use the spell-check on your e-mail application if it has one.

- **Think of column width.** Keep your e-mails to about 70 columns wide. If the width of your text extends beyond 80 columns, your message risks being broken up.
- **Check the address.** It can be quite a big PR mistake to send a private e-mail message to your entire mailing list.
- **Ask questions.** PR is about keeping relations alive, and by asking a question, you are ensuring a response.
- **Keep something back.** Never lay all your cards on the table. Keep some information back for future correspondence.
- **Be polite.** Never respond to unpleasant or aggressive messages in an unpleasant or aggressive manner. Always be polite and positive.

Salutations and signature files

Personal salutations (such as Dear Claire) at the beginning of messages are not necessary, and when the same message is sent to more than one person, they are not practical.

However, in terms of e-PR, a personal greeting is very effective. It lets the recipient know that the message was intended for him or her alone, and helps add a personal element to your relationship.

Signature files are a two- or three-line message at the foot of your e-mail. They tell the recipient who you are and what you do, typically including your name, job title, company name and Web site address. If you use Netscape Navigator or Microsoft's Internet Explorer, you can create a signature file using a Word program. Save it as a text file (not a Word file). It will then automatically be placed at the end of all your messages.

The Netscape command sequence goes 'Edit' – 'Preferences' – 'Identity'. A fill-in box then appears. Write your signature then click 'OK'. With Internet Explorer use the commands 'Options' – 'Signature' – 'Text' then type your signature and click 'OK'.

Layout

E-mail messages should be laid out with spaces in between each paragraph. By providing lots of spaces and short paragraphs, you are making the text appear more inviting and easier to read.

The golden rules of e-mail 'netiquette'

According to a recent survey, 58 per cent of companies feel that e-mail can cause misunderstanding and damage business relationships (Source: InTuition). The reason for this is that most people are not clear of the many pitfalls that can be encountered. To amend this situation, there now follows a rundown of the golden rules of e-mail 'netiquette' for standard e-mail messages:

- Make sure each message has a definite purpose – always ask, 'Do I need to send this message?'
- Ask questions to encourage a response and keep online relationships alive.
- Be friendly and polite.
- Avoid sending files and attachments. Many people cannot open them and those that can are reluctant to do so in the fear that they contain a virus.
- Avoid business jargon and blatant commercialism.
- Don't use HTML formatted files unless you know the recipient has an e-mail program that can read it.
- Be brief. Forget about the formalities of business letter writing. Aim for short sentences and lots of action verbs. Messages should never extend beyond 20 lines.
- Make subject lines specific and relevant.
- Respond to messages within 24 hours.
- Do not put anything in a message you would not want to get into the public domain or to be shown as legal evidence.
- Write in plain language. 'Please contact me if you have any questions' is a lot better than 'Should you require any further information, please do not hesitate. . .'

E-mail checklist

Before sending an e-mail message, check that you have:

- sent the message to the right person and address;
- made the message and subject line clear and relevant;
- protected any legally sensitive information;

- included a copyright notice if necessary;
- checked the accuracy of any facts or figures.

Summary

In order to get the full benefit of communicating via e-mail, a sound understanding of the basics is necessary. The purpose of this chapter has therefore been to inform or refresh you on the principles and practice of communicating in e-mail.

As a highly powerful communication tool, e-mail needs to be used sensitively when building one-to-one relations online. The next two chapters explore further the different uses e-mail can be put to in your e-PR programmes.

ten

Discussion **groups**

Once your Web site is up and running, you can reinforce your business profile and site address by monitoring and posting information to the two types of online discussion groups: newsgroups and mailing list discussion groups. There are over 30,000 individual newsgroups and many more mailing lists (discussion groups based on the e-mail system), which provide discussion forums covering every topic imaginable. Although newsgroups and mailing lists may cover the same subjects, the two work differently. Newsgroups, for instance, are open to everyone, whereas you need to subscribe to mailing lists by sending a message to a list server (e-mail software included in programs such as Microsoft's Outlook Express). This chapter will explain the benefits of incorporating newsgroups into your e-PR strategy.

The difference between newsgroups and mailing list discussion groups

Newsgroups provide an online forum, collectively referred to as Usenet. Usenet's thousands of discussion forums provide an arena in which people can say almost anything relating to the forum's specific subject areas. Most discussion groups are based on the e-mail system. These are called **mailing list discussion groups**. These groups are one of the most active parts of the Internet.

Although newsgroups and mailing lists are often grouped together under the collective term 'discussion groups', they operate in different ways.

The newsgroup difference

- Anyone can join a newsgroup.
- Articles are posted to a newsgroup using a newsreader.
- Users can follow the thread of a discussion group as messages are grouped with replies linked to the initial article.
- You can access a newsgroup using your Internet browser.
- Most major search engines index newsgroup contents.

The mailing list difference

- Mailing lists work by e-mail.
- To join a mailing list you subscribe by sending a message to a 'list server'.
- List servers automatically send messages to each member of the list.
- As messages are not stored, you cannot conduct content searches or follow discussions as easily as you can in a newsgroup.

Participation in these groups can be an extremely effective way of promoting your business. Businesses that succeed in this area of e-PR are those that promote their expertise rather than blatantly flaunt their products or services. The old cliché therefore still holds true in the age of new media: you only get out what you are willing to put in. Your success in a newsgroup is directly proportional to the amount of useful information you dispense. The logic works like this: if you provide people with useful answers to their questions, they will be receptive to learning more about your products or services.

Finding the right groups for your business

The first step is to find newsgroups and mailing lists that will be useful to your business. Specialist search engines and lists of the groups can be found at the following addresses:

- Liszt. – http://www.liszt.com/news/
- Deja. – http://dejanews.com/

- Tile.Net. – http:// www.tile.net
- Usenet Info Centre. – http://metalab.unc.edu/usenet-i/
- Yahoo!. – http://dir.yahoo.com/Computers_and_Internet/ Internet/ Usenet/Newsgroups_Listings

After entering keywords relevant to your target market into the search engines, you'll get a list back of messages that contain those keywords, along with the names of the discussion groups where they appear most frequently. This gives you a good indication of the best groups to explore. Read the description of the group and its code of conduct to see if new site announcements are welcomed or if the group is restricted to the realm of academic discussion.

Hang around

Before you start posting messages to discussion groups you should become a silent visitor for a while. That is to say, read the messages without taking an active part in the discussion. This will enable you to realize the way the group interacts, and you will get an idea of the sort of messages that will go down well and get the biggest response. You will also be able to make sure that the discussion group is appropriate for your purposes and that your messages will be reached by a relevant and considerable target audience.

To promote your business or site in discussion groups successfully takes considerable time and care. One of the biggest e-PR mistakes a business can make is to rush headlong into a group promoting your site and services without understanding the needs and interests of the group contributors. The key to success is to make relevant and occasional contributions that promote your expertise rather than flaunt your products or services.

Create a 'signature line'

A good 'signature line' is needed before posting messages (or 'articles', to give them their proper title), to discussion groups. A signature line is a sentence at the end of your message that says something about you, your business or your site.

The signature line offers space for blatant promotion unavailable in the message above. Providing the message above it is a valid contribution to the discussion group, your signature line will be great promotion for your business.

Signature lines are the acceptable face of free advertising on the Web. To my best knowledge, no one has ever been rebuked or 'flamed' for information about their Web site that they have included in their signature line.

It should be remembered, however, that the main purpose of a signature line is to provide contact information. Advertising your site must be seen as secondary.

Things to include in your signature

- the address of the Web page you want people who read the message to visit;
- your e-mail address, with a hypertext link;
- information on the latest developments on your site and on any forthcoming online events;
- contact details including telephone and fax numbers, a 'real world' address and your name;
- your company strapline;
- an indication of your position.

Keep messages in context

Newsgroups and mailing lists are established on the basis of a shared interest – be that accountancy, feng shui or horse riding. Therefore, when you participate in a discussion, make sure your message is relevant to the context. Don't try and sell your financial services in a group for book lovers. However, it is not just the topics of your messages that need to be in context, but also the tone.

Members of newsgroups generally want advice, not advertising. If you do want to use newsgroups in a blatantly commercial manner, there are newsgroups especially assigned for this purpose. In a normal newsgroup, leave the advertising for your signature line and stick with providing helpful and effective public relations in the body of the message.

To keep your messages in context:

- Keep them relevant to the subject topic.
- Be commercial in the right places – in your signature line and in commercial newsgroups such as E-mail Promote (http://www.emailpromote.listbot.com).
- Quote from the message you are responding to.

When to post

As important a question as what to post, is the issue of when to post. The first rule is only post occasionally when you have something of value to offer. Perhaps even more importantly, never post the same message to more than one group, as readers of one group are likely to read others. If you are caught doing this, your attempt at successful e-PR has turned into a clumsy and ineffective ad campaign.

Advisors

Once you get to know a group you will discover that out of an audience of, say, 1,000 group members there are usually only 50 or so people who regularly post messages. Within this smaller group, there is an even smaller circle of about 10 to 15 who are group **advisors**. These people respond quickly to questions and provide the most authoritative answers. Such is their reputation, often messages are addressed to them by name. This is the position of authority you want to be in. Successful e-PR will lead you to the top of the discussion group hierarchy, and to a position in which others in the group will be promoting you (and, by association, your business site) on your behalf. Once in this position you will have to choose very carefully the questions and queries you respond to, to maintain your advisory role.

Volunteer to become a sysop (system operator)

If you want to have even greater influence within a newsgroup, you can apply to become part of the group's administration as a system operator. If you think of a topic you know well that will have an ongoing appeal on a relevant message board, post your suggestion to the moderator of the newsgroup. This is a particularly good idea if you are a consultant or advisor, as it will allow you to demonstrate your expertise from a position of authority.

Handling complaints

One of your tasks should be to monitor the groups and reply promptly and politely to any complaints, problems or sensitive issues voiced about your company. An immediate, personal response shows that your company is ready to listen to complaints and do something about it. For instance, if a product doesn't work, respond by saying that you have passed this on to the technical or manufacturing department of your business.

Try and isolate complaints and get a one-to-one dialogue going with the unhappy customers. Remember, it is far better that they complain to you than to other members of your target market.

By visiting one of the discussion group search engines (see above), and typing in your company or brand name, you can keep abreast of any negative remarks about your business. This issue will be discussed in more detail in the next chapter.

Writing messages

You will need to read a lot of postings – many lists generate hundreds of messages every day – to check for messages that ask questions that enable you to show off your expertise.

Furthermore, if you want people to visit your site, you have to write messages as a real person rather than as a sales representative. While giving advice, also ask questions to engage people in ongoing discussion. These questions can relate to your business, such as:

Have you any useful ideas for people we could invite to answer questions in our discussion group?
or
Are there any services/products you would like to see us provide?

Answer questions

The best way to build up credibility in discussion groups is to provide useful answers to questions. Even if the question doesn't directly relate to your business, answering it will benefit you in the following ways:

- People will see your business information in your signature line.
- You will be appreciated for providing something free.
- You will build up your reputation as a good 'netizen' (online citizen) and be in a better position to promote your business when the right opportunity arises.

Contribute without answering questions

If you cannot find any relevant questions that would allow you to show off your expertise, it is still possible to contribute in the following ways:

- Post an advice article (or 'Ten Top Tips' on something).
- Ask a question that will help you conduct market research.

The dos and don'ts of newsgroup 'netiquette'

To use newsgroups and mailing lists successfully you need to be aware of the dos and don'ts of online etiquette, or 'netiquette':

DO:

- Keep messages relevant. If the topic is wine don't respond with information about your accountancy service.
- Make sure your messages are kept short (no longer than 200 words) as people have a lot of messages to read through.
- Build credibility by answering questions that don't relate directly to your business.

■ Be polite, informative and friendly.
■ Get to know the dynamics of a group before you post a message.

DON'T

■ Send the same message to more than one newsgroup simultaneously.
■ Clog up the newsgroup with 'thank you' messages. Use the TIA ('thanks in advance') abbreviation in your initial message.
■ Get your friends to write questions like 'can you recommend a good wine merchant?' if you are a wine merchant.

Create your own mailing list

If you want to make sure that the discussion groups you contribute to are directly relevant to your business, you can create your own mailing list. This way you can build and consolidate relationships with your various target audiences. Owning your own list means the material you post can be more promotional. You can post company information, tell people about your site, answer questions and let people discuss among themselves.

To create your own list you need to:

■ Work with an ISP that has software enabling you to manage the mailing functions and track subscriptions. Listproc, Listserv and Majordomo are the three main mailing list software programs.
■ Place a welcome message at the list's home page detailing the subject the list covers, who should join and any rules or regulations you feel are necessary.

To attract members:

■ post announcement messages in other discussion groups;
■ refer to the mailing list in your signature line;
■ provide subscription forms on your company Web site;
■ promote the mailing list in newsletters, adverts, etc.

Your mailing list can either be **active** (where you and your subscribers can post messages) or **passive** (where only you can post messages). Active lists allow you less control but can be more useful as they enable you to gauge the opinions of your audiences.

People should always know before they subscribe how they can unsubscribe. A typical announcement message could therefore look like this:

> *To subscribe to Tropical Fish List send an e-mail to list@tropicalfishworld.com with a blank subject line and a message body of 'subscribe tropical'. To unsubscribe change the message body to 'unsubscribe tropical'.*

Summary

Contributing to discussion groups can be one of the most effective and personal ways of communicating your business message to new audiences. A great deal of sensitivity is needed, however, to build up trust in these groups. Many business people use these groups in a manner so clumsy that they give the group, as well as themselves, a bad name. If you push your business too hard in a newsgroup or mailing list, you suffer the humiliation of being flamed. That is to say, you will receive protest from all the other members who do not appreciate such direct promotional tactics. Many people have used them to great effect, particularly to promote themselves as specialists in their business area. This form of e-PR takes time and patience required to carry it out successfully but due to the interactive and indirect nature of communicating your business message in this context, the rewards can be immense.

eleven

Online **newsletters**

As we have already discussed, your e-PR effort must extend beyond the Web. Discussion groups are one obvious way to generate interest in your business or Web site, but may not be so good for maintaining interest. To build long-term relations with your various audiences, you should consider the numerous benefits of putting together an informative e-mail newsletter.

Online v offline newsletters

Online or offline newsletters can be a fantastic PR tool as they enable you to bypass a third party (such as a journalist) and communicate with your publics directly. The advantages online newsletters have over their offline counterparts, however, are immense. Some of these advantages include:

- **Cost.** The considerable printing and postage costs involved in distributing newsletters offline are avoided altogether online.
- **Interactivity.** Online newsletters can be made interactive through HTML links and can therefore **involve** the reader to a greater extent than they could offline. You can therefore use them to build two-way, as opposed to one-way relationships.
- **Time.** Although online newsletters require you to invest a considerable amount of time in putting them together, they can be distributed simultaneously to thousands of people in an instant.

Clarify your objectives

Before you decide the format or frequency of your newsletter, you need to be sure of your objectives. What do you want it to achieve?

Online newsletters can be used to:

- Generate return visits to your Web site. Attracting a link to your site and including extracted articles from your site are two tried and tested ways of using online newsletters to encourage repeat site traffic.
- Boost your reputation. By providing informative and objective articles of interest to clients, customers and even competitors, you can enhance your reputation as an authority on your business area.
- Gauge interest in your Web site. If you have a page of your site with information about and a subscription form for your newsletter, you will be able to get an idea of not only how many people visit your site, but of how many people have a strong interest in your site and business messages. By subscribing to a newsletter, visitors are volunteering, in effect, to engage in some form of relationship with your business.
- Create a mailing list. Newsletters provide you with the perfect incentive for visitors to your Web site to provide you with their e-mail addresses.

Of course, newsletters can be and often are used for a combination of all the above reasons to great effect.

Content

To use an online newsletter as an effective e-PR tool, you need to see it as a way of forging mutually beneficial relations between you and your public. To do this you have to understand why people go online, and why they would subscribe to an online newsletter. It certainly isn't to be bombarded with sales jargon or flash adverts for your company. No, the reason most people go online is to find answers to questions and solutions to problems, whether they look for these via the Web, discussion groups or e-mail. If people subscribe to an online newsletter, they therefore want information, not to read your strap line and mission statement a thousand times over.

Successful newsletters are about your audience, not your company. Of course, you should write about your company but only where it is of direct interest to people who buy your products. If you sell jazz CDs, for instance, your newsletter could include features on different jazz artists, forthcoming jazz festivals as well as occasional reviews of new additions to your stock list.

If you are in the service sector, the content could follow a guide format, offering free advice to establish your expertise. Consider the type of information you can give away. If you are an accountancy firm, your newsletter could include tips on how to manage your accounts as well as other pearls of financial wisdom.

Many people feel hesitant about giving away the secrets of their success, but this is the wrong attitude to have regarding the Internet. It may sound obvious but to be valued in the information age you need to provide valuable information. Only by giving away something useful can you make a name for yourself online.

Other ideas for your newsletter content:

- Ask for suggestions. Another way of making sure a newsletter is relevant to your target audience is to invite subscribers to contribute suggestions for feature articles. This also adds a further interactive element to your newsletter.
- If your newsletter is used to promote your Web site, include at least one extract from your site in each issue, alongside links to new features on your site.
- Include links to articles on other relevant sites.
- Use Web site material.
- Include a question and answer page. Again, this will help strengthen the point of contact between you and your audience.
- Incorporate company information into a news section informing people of new developments, refinements in products or services, new ways to use your product or service, awards you pick up and so on. Try and present company news in as objective a manner as possible (see below).

Make your newsletter objective

Successful relationships with your audience are based on two things: providing something people want and establishing trust. To do both of these things with your newsletter you need to make it as objective as possible.

In someone else's publication, whether online or offline, the PR aim is to get as many mentions of your company in as possible. In your own publication, the opposite is almost true. The more your company product or service name is referred to, the more authority over your audience you lose. While you must ensure subscribers are fully aware that the newsletter is your business publication, you need to limit any blatant bias towards your company.

Traditionally, successful PR comes through third-party endorsement. People are more likely to believe your business is great if someone else tells them – be they a journalist, a trusted friend or public figure.

By definition, third-party endorsement is not completely possible from a communication tool, such as an online newsletter, that you produce yourself. However, a degree of objectivity can still be achieved. Here are some ways to increase the value of your newsletter by rendering it more objective:

- Send out an e-mail to relevant journalists asking if they would be willing to write an article for your newsletter.
- Ask for suggestions from subscribers via e-mail.
- Don't use the name of your business in the title of your newsletter. My own online newsletter, for instance, is called 'Online PR Guide' with the subtitle 'A Peppermint PR publication' conceding its business intention.
- Ask to 'borrow' material from other sources: magazines; e-zines; Web sites; other newsletters and so on.
- Stick to material relevant to your business area, rather than your business interest.
- Gather feedback from subscribers via e-mail and incorporate some of the more favourable comments into the newsletter.
- Include a question and answer page. Getting subscribers to e-mail questions provides you with a legitimate platform from which to soft sell your business.

Size is not important

There is no hard and fast rule as to how long your online newsletter should be. Indeed, less can often prove to be more. One or two articles, a question and answer page, and a brief 'Note from the Editor', together totalling 1,500 words may prove to be enough. After all, you do not want to frighten off your subscribers by burdening them with too much information. The danger with long newsletters is that, regardless of how useful they are, they have a tendency to get deleted before they are read. Then again, if you have a loyal readership, a longer newsletter may prove more worthwhile as people may want to print the newsletter. If you are unsure about the most suitable length for your newsletter, you could e-mail some of your subscribers to ask their opinion.

Frequency

Just as the issue of length is dependent on the nature of your company and audience, so too is the question of how frequently you should put your newsletter out. Indeed, the frequency of your newsletter will probably depend on its length. If your newsletter's length is worthy of Leo Tolstoy it probably isn't a good idea to send it out on a daily, or even weekly, basis.

If numerous people share publishing duties then obviously you can send out a newsletter more often than if you compile it single-handedly. Another point you should take into consideration is that, however useful your newsletter is, people generally don't have the time to read an entire newsletter every day.

I personally find that sending out a newsletter monthly strikes the right balance between feeling too pressured and forgetting about it.

Format

When laying out your newsletter there are some basic rules to follow to make it more effective:

- Place spaces between paragraphs to make the text easier to read.
- Keep columns under 70 characters long.
- Don't centre your text. The newsletter will appear differently on different e-mail programs so don't try and centre or justify your text as it may look drastically different on someone else's computer screen.

- Avoid 'monospace' font. 'Monospace' fonts, such as Arial and Courier, are fonts in which every letter takes up the same amount of space. The fonts look entirely different on each e-mail software program.
- Remember to spell-check your newsletter.
- Send the newsletter to yourself. Before you send out your newsletter, send a copy to yourself or a colleague to check that it looks alright. The header of your newsletter should read:

Content –Type: text/palin;charset='iso-8859–1'

This means your newsletter will look the same on different e-mail programs.

Distribution

When it comes to distributing a newsletter online, you have two options: do it yourself or pay for a company to do it for you.

Do it yourself

The main advantages of distributing a newsletter yourself include:

- **Control.** You have complete control over when your newsletter is issued as well as over who receives it.
- **Cost.** Doing it yourself is clearly the cheapest option.

The potential disadvantages of distributing a newsletter yourself include:

- **Time.** Distributing a newsletter takes a lot of time, particularly when you have a large subscriber base.
- **Complexity.** If you have over 300 subscribers, you are letting yourself in for a complicated administrative task. The mere act of adding and removing subscribers becomes, in itself, a considerable chore.

To distribute an online newsletter yourself you need to create your own subscriber list of e-mail addresses. For this you will need a software program, such as Pegasus (http://www.pegasus.usa.com/) that can filter addresses in and out of the address book. Major e-mail programs like Eudora Pro 4.1 and Outlook 2000 are unable to do this.

You *can* collect a subscriber list of e-mail addresses using these systems; it's just that the task is a lot more difficult without the aid of a sophisticated e-mail filtering tool. To collect e-mail addresses from your Web site you need to set up a subscription form which links to your e-mail system. The easiest way to do this is by using a 'WYSIWYG' ('what you see is what you get') Web building tool such as Adobe Page Mill, Microsoft Front Page or Dreamweaver, which will do the technical stuff for you (see Figure 11.1).

However, when you first set up your newsletter you may find it more straightforward to get people to e-mail their contact details to you.

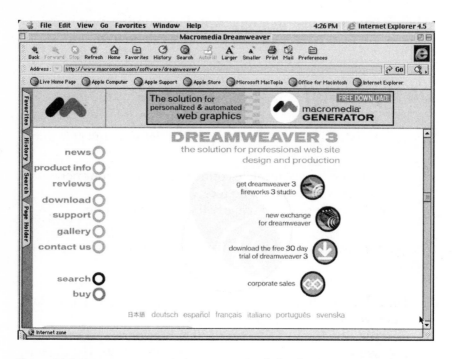

Figure 11.1 Dreamweaver can help you set subscription forms up on your site without using HTML codes

Getting people to sign up

The best and most obvious place to promote your newsletter is on your Web site, as people will be able to sign up then and there. Whether you opt for a subscription form or simply ask people to e-mail their information to you, make sure you do the following:

- Make it clear that any information people give you will remain confidential and not sold on to mailing list companies.
- Keep the information required down to a minimum. People are put off when faced with lengthy forms to fill in.
- Make it easy for people to unsubscribe by providing an 'unsubscribe' option on your form, or by telling people they can unsubscribe by sending you an e-mail saying 'I want to unsubscribe'.
- Give details of the next issue date and indicate the frequency of the newsletter.
- Provide a sample extract from the current newsletter on the subscription page.
- Indicate who the newsletter is aimed at and will appeal to as well as who has helped put it together. It is a good idea to allow at least two months for people to subscribe before the first issue date, to allow you to build up a substantial list of e-mail addresses.

Promoting your online newsletter

As well as publicizing your online newsletter on your Web Site, you should promote it on other online media. There are a number of search engines that cater specifically for newsletters and e-zines. Here are the main ones:

- E-Zines Z. – http://www.e-zinez.com
- InfoBot. – http://www.infobot.net
- Liszt. – http://www.liszt.com

Another way to promote your newsletter is to encourage subscribers to pass the newsletter on to people they feel would appreciate it, and then include a copyright notice.

Posting your online newsletter

Whatever e-mail software you use, the chances are that you will be able to send to multiple e-mail addresses simultaneously.

The way to do this properly involves using that great e-PR tool, the Bcc: line. If you enter all the addresses into the To: or Cc: text boxes you will breach the rules of e-mail netiquette as each recipient of the newsletter will be able to see the e-mail address of every other recipient.

By using the Bcc: box you will be able to preserve the confidentiality of your subscription list, and avoid frustrating your subscribers by sending them a page full of e-mail addresses.

However, some programs will not allow you to use the Bcc: box alone as they will not send a message without an address in the To: line as well. The best thing to do in this case is to put your own address in the To: text box and send a copy of the newsletter to yourself.

Using a service to post your newsletter

The ascending interest in sending out online newsletters has led to the provision of free services by companies (such as ListBot http://www. listbot.com) that distribute the newsletter for you in exchange for placing advertising within the newsletter. I would advise you to make sure, however, that the mailing list the newsletter is distributed to is relevant to your business.

If you do decide to use a service, it is probably safer to pay for a service program such as Lyris (http://www.lyris.net) or Sparklist (http://www. sparklist.com). These programs are particularly useful if the size of your newsletter and subscriber base is large, as they allow you to personalize each newsletter automatically (by incorporating the subscriber's name into each message). Other advantages include:

- A 'split' feature. A split feature allows you to send different newsletters to different sections of your list.
- The ability to send messages automatically at pre-ordained times.

▓ The provision of detailed delivery reports, telling you how many newsletters were sent out and how many 'bounced' back.

To pay for these services you have two options. You can either pay for the software program outright or pay monthly for the service (the more cost-effective option, at least in the short- to mid-term).

Newsletter or e-zine

Another way to add authority to your online newsletter is to convert it into an e-zine. Although there is some overlap in the definitions of online newsletters and e-zines, there are some identifiable differences:

▓ Typically, an e-zine is longer with a minimum of, say, 20 pages.
▓ E-zines are often Web-based and therefore written in HTML code script. Online newsletters are written mainly using plain text, with links alone being converted in HTML; as a result e-zines have a tendency to be colourful and interactive.
▓ E-zines are often available at a URL (Web site address) as well as sent via e-mail, whereas newsletters are usually distributed via e-mail alone.

E-zines can be a worthwhile alternative to an online newsletter as they can provide your audiences with a glossier and lengthier source of information. However, e-zines will cost you more in terms of time, money and human resources than an online newsletter. Furthermore, e-zines are distributed via HTML mail (e-mail messages that are formatted using HTML coding), which is incompatible with some e-mail programs. Unless you are certain every subscriber has an e-mail program that can translate HTML, you should stick to a plain text newsletter.

Virtual-Festivals

The successful portal site Virtual-Festivals (http://www.virtual-festivals.com) that enables people around the world to experience major summer pop and rock music festivals 'virtually', uses an electronic newsletter to involve visitors as frequently as possible. The newsletter provides updates about upcoming festivals and concerts, as well as announcing when new live audiovisual content is added to the site. Virtual-Festivals provides genuine incentives to subscribe by creating competitions offering users the chance to win CDs, videos and signed artist photos that can only be accessed by newsletter subscribers.

As Virtual-Festivals centres on the summer season, founders Steve Jenner and Simon Roberts felt an online newsletter would be the perfect way to build relationships with users all year round. With an ever-increasing number of international subscribers, they have been proved right.

Despite the colourful and dynamic visual emphasis on the Virtual-Festivals Web site, the newsletter is distributed in plain text (as opposed to HTML) so that all subscribers can access the newsletter, regardless of the e-mail software they use (see Figure 11.2).

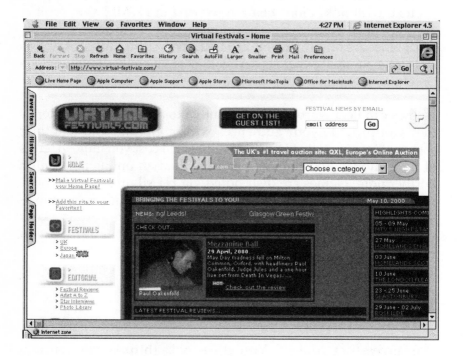

Figure 11.2 The Virtual-Festivals home page

Summary

Sending out an online newsletter can bring you closer to the people who matter to your business, by issuing useful information into individual mailboxes. As with discussion groups, newsletters allow you to demonstrate your expertise and promote your business as a result. However, as with your contributions to discussion groups, great care is needed to keep your messages relevant to the requirements of your target audience; after all, e-PR is about building relations, not the hard sell. People are very sensitive over the issue of e-mail and get frustrated over anything irrelevant that is sent to their mailbox, even if they have a subscription. That said, providing they are centred on the interests of your audience, online newsletters will prove to be beneficial to your business, keeping relationships alive.

Internal **e-PR**

As we have already discussed, the Internet can be used in many ways to boost your relations with external audiences: customers, consumers, competitors, investors, journalists, search engines and so on. It can also be used, however, to improve the relationship and communications between your business and its internal audience of employees.

Good internal relations depend on an organization's desire and ability to engage in a dialogue with its employees. Organizations that are willing to share information with their workforce, and that are able to listen to the response, tend to function more successfully as they are able to present to the outside world a clearer picture of who they are and what they stand for.

Web sites and internal relations

Web sites can be used to boost employee relations in a number of ways. One technique used by many businesses online is to involve staff in the process of developing the Web sites. You could conduct a survey asking employees what they think should be included on the Web site. This can serve a double purpose. It can make employees feel more involved in the decision-making process, as well as helping you produce a site that is truly reflective of your company.

Another way to get staff involved with your Web sites is to put members of staff *on* your site. Don't just include profiles of the managerial staff; put the employees on there too. Asda (http://www.asda.com), for instance, includes members of its shop staff on the site in the role of 'site guides', helping visitors navigate their way around the Web sites. You can draw on your staff's expertise by getting them involved in 'Question and

Answer' pages and by contributing to your site's discussion area. You could even have a page of your site dedicated to staff news. There are many other ways you can use your Web sites to involve your staff; all it needs is a little imagination.

Internal online newsletters

Online newsletters, which are discussed in detail elsewhere, can be a way of strengthening relations with employees. Online or offline, internal newsletters can keep employees informed of changes and events that may be of interest. The sort of information that can be incorporated into a newsletter includes:

- General company news: mergers; partnerships; acquisitions; market shares; sponsorships; expansion plans; buyouts, business wins; new products; competitors, and so on. These can all be reported to employees via a newsletter.
- New appointments. Employees can be kept informed of any new start appointments.
- Training courses. Include news of any staff training opportunities.
- Holiday timetables.
- Staff promotions.
- Staff news. Newsletters should be *about* as well as *for* your staff. Be imaginative; don't just take the standard 'births, marriages and deaths' line.
- Internal vacancies.

The significant advantage of internal newsletters sent over the Internet is that they can be more interactive, and therefore involve employees more. Sending internal newsletters via e-mail is more likely to encourage a response.

Internal e-mail

E-mail is the most significant internal e-PR tool of all. It provides a quick and efficient way for people to communicate within an organization. It has made the distribution of information and ideas between departments and (in international organizations) different countries simpler and has enabled all members of the workforce to get involved with the process.

The reasons why e-mail has become such an effective method of internal communication include:

- **Cost.** A business manager based in London can communicate with colleagues based in New York or Sydney for (at the most) the same price as a local phone call.
- **Convenience.** Every member of your business can be contacted simultaneously via e-mail.
- **Feedback.** E-mail provides more introverted members of staff with a way of bringing up issues that they would feel too awkward to talk about face-to-face or over the phone.
- **Access.** As technology advances e-mail is fast becoming accessible (to quote Martini's famous strap line) 'anyplace, anywhere, anytime'. Laptops, palmtops, mobile phones and other gadgets are enabling organizations to keep in contact with their 'field staff' 24 hours a day.
- **Adaptability.** Internal reports, spreadsheets, proposals, agendas, designs, timetables, reminders and other material can all be sent via e-mail.

As business models become increasingly horizontal and as internal dialogue starts to replace the old-fashioned 'I command, you obey' paradigm, e-mail seems to have arrived at the right time. E-mail is a fast, convenient, easy-to-use, low-cost way of communicating internally and businesses should use it effectively.

Compiling an internal e-mailing list

To use e-mail effectively you should compile an e-mailing list of all employees, then break it down into sub-categories relating to individual departments (eg human resource, finance and marketing). If your organization is geographically spread out, you could also have sub-categories relating to different locations (eg London, New York, Sydney). This will enable you to send each specific internal audience messages exclusively of relevance to them, as well as sending the entire workforce e-mail messages all at once.

Intranets

Intranets are, to all intents and purposes, internal Internets. They use exactly the same technology as Internets but operate within the confines of a private local network (LAN). Intranets allow an organization to have its own private 'Web' of sites used only by its users. In addition, they can also be used for e-mail purposes for internal messages between the members of the private network.

The benefits of using an Intranet for your internal relations are immense. Here are some of the reasons why you should consider converting to an Intranet:

- **Security.** Intranets provide all the benefits of the Internet with the added advantage of security. Whereas everything you do on the Internet can be accessed by virtually anyone (which is why all online activity is e-PR activity) on an Intranet you can keep messages confidential without the risk of an investigative journalist or hostile competitor having a look.
- **Target audience.** Intranets enable you to target your messages to an internal audience without having to consider your relations with other audiences.
- **E-mail traffic.** An Intranet can help reduce the volume of internal e-mail traffic. Internal departments can have their own sites and so up-to-date information can be provided in security without the need to send e-mail messages.
- **Cost.** As the Internet started as an academic (as opposed to commercial) network, there is a strong tradition of cheap and cooperative Internet technology. In fact, a lot of Internet software is free. Among the valuable freebies are Apache (the most popular Web server), and the e-mail software programs Pegasus and Eudora.
- **Variety.** As well as enabling you to have your own Web and e-mail systems, an Intranet can support chat, Usenet and other Internet services. You can set up newsgroups to encourage people to share information within departments or across your organization.
- **Growth.** Intranets can grow with your business.

Intranets have started to revolutionize internal communications by making information more secure and yet at the same time easier to access for those who need it. Furthermore, while Internet users cannot access your Intranet, you can access the Internet via your Intranet. People within your company can use one e-mail program to exchange messages with both Intranet and Internet users.

The fact that each department within your business can create its own Web sites can also benefit your internal e-PR efforts. Instead of circulating memos by hand, each department can announce information on its site. For example, your finance, marketing and sales departments can look at information on one another's Web sites to help decide pricing policies.

Every department can post Web pages to share its information with the departments in your business.

Security issues

If you decide to connect your Intranet to the Internet, you will need to control the type of information that can pass between the two systems. After all, if confidential company information gets into the wrong hands, you could end up having to manage a crisis. The technology, which helps provide unlimited access, constitutes a **firewall** (named after the barrier that prevents a fire from spreading from a car engine into the passenger compartment). Firewalls can help you restrict Internet access to e-mail only as well as control what can log into the Intranet.

As well as using firewall technology, you will also need to take steps to ensure that the Intranet is used appropriately within your business. To do this you will need to:

- Establish a user policy – e-mail rules and guidelines for using the Intranet to all your employees.
- Monitor activity. Although the e-PR aim is to encourage a free flow of information within an organization, you will still need to ensure that someone is responsible for the content of the Intranet's Web sites and newsgroups.
- Limit usage to current employees only. This means that when someone leaves to go elsewhere his or her Intranet account should be closed.

Furthermore, it is worth taking into consideration that information on an Intranet can be only *so* secure. After all, your employees do have contact with the outside world. This doesn't mean you should be paranoid; it just means you need to be careful.

As well as these security issues, you should also remember that, although an Intranet can be the answer to all your internal PR needs, people will need to be educated on how to use it effectively. Users will need to be given e-mail and Web training as well as given instruction on how to use newsgroups and so on. They will need to know how to create Web pages, manage mailing lists and create and maintain other Intranet resources if the Intranet is to be an e-PR success.

Summary

To communicate a clear and consistent positive message outside your organization, it is important to encourage the free flow of communication within your organization. The Internet and Intranet technology can help bring an organization closer together by enabling people to interact with one another frequently and efficiently. It can also help generate mutual understanding between different internal departments via e-mail or Intranet-based newsgroups and Web pages.

thirteen

E-media **relations**

On the Internet all your activity is, by definition, media activity as the Internet is a form of media. However, 'media relations' refers to third-party media that are beyond your immediate control.

This chapter explores the ways you can influence the online journalists and editors who influence your audiences. Although many of the methods in this chapter apply equally to targeting online and offline media, the emphasis is on techniques that are particularly suited to e-media.

Third-party e-media

Third-party e-media is a term used to describe any media on the Internet beyond you and your business's control. It does not include your Web site, e-mail messages, online newsletters, discussion group contributions and so on. However, it does include other Web sites, e-zines, journals and third-party newsletters.

Web sites

There are various types of sites that are useful to target during an e-media campaign. These include online versions of print publications, news sites and trade sites (which cover news stories relating to your business area).

E-zines

An e-zine is an online magazine. There are literally thousands of e-zines out there covering as diverse a range of topics (if not more diverse) as traditional magazines. As e-zines tend to be updated far more regularly than their offline cousins, the opportunities for coverage are often greater. A well-written press release is seen as a more valuable commodity online than it is in the real world. Salon (http://www.salonmagazine.com) is generally esteemed the biggest and best of the e-zine breed (see Figure 13.1).

Journals

Online journals are similar to e-zines except they tend to be more academically orientated. In addition, they often provide a lower level of interactivity and are updated less frequently.

Third-party newsletters

Other organizations' online newsletters are another form of e-media worth targeting. Many newsletters cover topics relevant to

Figure 13.1 The Salon e-zine is the publication by which all other e-zines are measured

an industry sector rather than the narrow interests of the organization itself. Your trade organizations or amicable competitors may be willing to write about your company or (as is more likely to be the case) welcome a feature article written by you or a colleague.

The right media for the right audience

The first thing you need to decide is which are the specific audiences you want to hear your message. This will help you dictate the type of e-media you want to target. If, for instance, you have just won some form of recognition by your industry, your target audience could be your competition. To reach your competitors your main target would be the relevant trade sites, e-zines and newsletters.

Researching the media

To find relevant online publications you can search the main search engines. Yahoo! conveniently has a list of all the online media directories (http://www.yahoo.com/News_and_Media/WebDirectories/). Amongst the most user-friendly e-media directories, you have Media Finder (http://www.mediafinder.com) for international e-media and Media UK (http://www.mediauk.com) (see Figure 13.2).

The single most useful site for finding different types of e-media is NewJour (http://www.newjour.com). This site indexes new and archived newsletters, e-zines and journals, many of which are not indexed elsewhere. Its easy-to-use search facility enables you to search its vast database by alphabetical category or keyword search.

When discriminating between different online publications you should look for the following:

■ Publications that mention your competitors. If they already write about your competition, there is a strong chance they will consider writing about you.
■ Features that relate to issues associated with your site.
■ Material relevant to your audiences. If the site does not appeal to any section of your target market, there is little point seeking coverage.

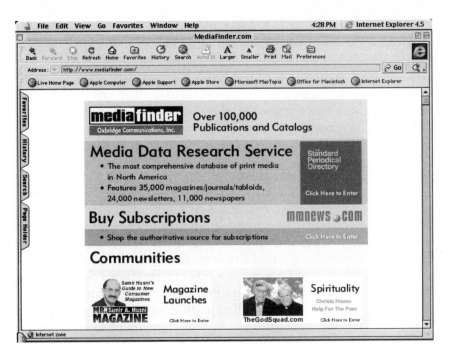

Figure 13.2 Media Finder is one of the most comprehensive online media directories

Once you have researched your target media, and found the appropriate angle to gain publicity, you are then ready to send your story out into cyberspace. This chapter will look at how to build up contact with e-journalists and the different ways you can let them know about news relating to your site and business.

Finding the contacts

If you are already aware of the e-journalists you want to contact, look at their contributions to see if they have put their e-mail address at the foot of their piece. If they have not you could e-mail the publication and ask. As you find more and more relevant contact details you can build your own personalized media contact list.

To speed up the process you can supplement your own additions with lists from online media directories. Sites such as Media

UK (http://www.mediauk.com) and FAIR (http://www.fair.org) include e-mail addresses alongside other media contact information (see Figure 13.3).

Also, Peter Gugerell's E-mail Media List (http://www.ping.at/gugerell/media/e2indx.htm) is an excellent, although little known resource which has a huge list of e-mail addresses for online and offline media across the globe.

Approaching journalists

If you want a mention in a relevant e-zine, contact the editor and see if he or she would be interested in an article on or from you and your business. Offer a reciprocal exchange in any newsletter or e-zines you publish. One of the easiest ways to get publicity for yourself is to offer it to someone else. Even if you don't have a newsletter you might be able to offer a link to their site. However, even if you are unable or unwilling to offer anything in return, there is no reason why you should not be able to gain online coverage. If

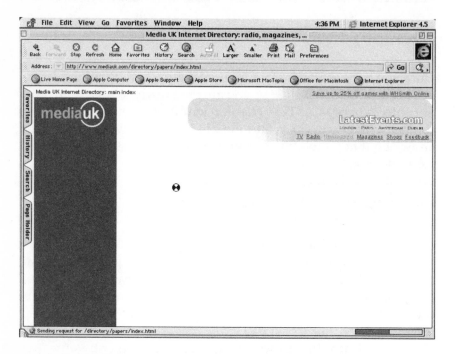

Figure 13.3 Media UK indexes e-mail and other media contact details

the information you are offering is fit enough to be called 'news' and the publications you target are relevant, you shouldn't have a problem. Provide a strong, interesting story, and the e-media will recognize the value of your business, and report accordingly. All you need to do now is to put together an e-media release.

Avoiding 'snooze news'

'Snooze news' consists of stories many companies feel should make the headlines, but in fact end up sending journalists to sleep. The most frequent examples of 'snooze news' include:

- **The new site story.** In 1995 when the Web was just beginning to be populated by commerce, a business that launched a new Web site would legitimately expect to gain media coverage. In the new millennium, however, the launch of a new Web site will not send an editor's pulse racing unless it breaks a world record or is endorsed by a royal.
- **The upgraded site story.** If anything, a site upgrade has a higher snooze factor than a site launch. Site makeovers have virtually no appeal outside the Internet magazine market.
- **The 'my site is popular' story.** A high hit rate or sudden surge in site visitors does not guarantee media interest. A site is expected to attract visitors, that is its *raison d'être*, and so site popularity alone does not qualify as a newsworthy story.

When publicizing your site in the online media you need to think in terms of how your site helps the audience who visit it. Find a way of demonstrating the unique or *unusual* benefits of your site. There is an old PR adage that holds true for the new media: 'If a dog bites a man no one cares, but if a man bites a dog it is news'. No one is interested in normality; to make waves you need to think of ways to turn the status quo on its head.

Grabbing attention

For all the differences between the online and the offline media, the ways to grab the editor's attention remain the same. Here are some pointers to think about when putting the spin to a site or business story:

- **People power.** News must be about people, connected to people or affect people in some way.
- **Be topical.** Making your Web site have a topical angle is one way to increase your chances of media coverage. Perhaps you could hold an online debate about a current issue of national or international concern.
- **Be first.** If your site is the first to do something, it is more likely to have media appeal.
- **Be controversial.** As mentioned above, controversy is one sure-fire way to make a splash.
- **Reveal benefits.** Think of ways your site could have a real impact on the lives of its visitors.
- **Conduct a survey**. As mentioned earlier in this book, research can be a very effective publicity tool as the results can be published across a range of media.
- **Hold an event.** Holding an imaginative online or offline event can help your site or business get a mention in the media.
- **Be environmental.** The Internet is an environmentally friendly medium. Think of a way your online activity helps the environment.
- **Awards**. Both giving and receiving awards can generate publicity and can boost your 'authority' status.
- **Partnerships**. Merger, sponsorship and partnership deals attract coverage by combining the weight of your business with someone else's.

Putting together an e-media release

An e-media release can be used to target offline as well as online publications. The difference is, however, that online publications expect you to send an e-media release, whereas most offline publications still prefer you to send a printed press release as well (although this situation is beginning to change).

The guidelines concerning the format of an e-media release overlap with those of a printed press release. The following points apply equally to both online and offline releases:

- Announce 'MEDIA RELEASE' clearly at the top of the page.
- Keep releases short (two pages maximum).
- Make your headline identify the story in less than five words.
- Put the date on the release at the top, clearly visible.
- Keep sentences short and succinct.
- Clarify the main points of your story (who? when? where? what? how much? and so on) in the opening paragraph. Then proceed with decreasingly significant details.
- Use quotes (preferably from third parties).
- Use the word 'ENDS' at the bottom right-hand corner of the release.
- Place contact information at the foot of the release. This should be preceded by 'For further information contact:' and should include your name, e-mail address and telephone number.

For e-media releases, however, you should also adhere to the following advice:

- Use links. Include e-mail links for each contact person and include hyperlinks to online reports, company profiles and any other relevant background information. You should also include a link to your site.
- Use Microsoft Word or WordPerfect to create your release, then transfer it to an HTML file before you send it.
- Add each release to an archive of releases accessible via your site.

To get an idea of how other people put press releases together, look at Yahoo!'s impressive Press Release page (http://www.yahoo.com/Business_and_Economy/Companies/News_and_Media/News_Services/Press_Releases/). This page links to various release services, where you will find many different release types of varying standards.

Distributing releases

When you are distributing releases to the online media, simply 'cut' and 'paste' the relevant e-mail addresses from your database and transfer them into the Bcc: box. Remember not to use the To: or Cc:

boxes unless you want to tell everyone on the list the addresses of everyone you have sent to.

The one advantage of sending releases to online media is that the traditional PR concern over deadline dates is all but eliminated.

Contribute articles

At times when your site has nothing to shout about there is still a way to gain coverage in e-zines and newsletters: write an article. Indeed, because online media are often updated on a daily basis, there are more opportunities for you to get an article published on the Internet than in the 'real world'.

Writing an article on your business area or an issue relevant to your site, with your name and business details given at the bottom, can prove to be very effective. It can help you boost your status as an authority in your business sector, and therefore make it more likely that e-journalists will contact you for a quote or comment when they next write something relating to your business. Furthermore, editors of offline publications often trawl the e-zines looking for inspiring articles they can use in their magazine or trade journal.

The articles that cause the biggest stir are those that court a little bit of controversy. As an over-hyped trend starts to lose steam, site editors want another angle. If you can provide it, you're in! In fact, controversy tends to be even more welcome on the Internet than it is offline.

When you have an idea for a suitable article, e-mail the relevant editor or Webmaster and ask if he or she is interested. Explain who you are and tell him or her why you think it would be appropriate for his or her audience. If he or she likes the article and it proves a success, it is likely you will be commissioned to produce more of the same.

Become a media source

The ultimate aim of your relations with the media (online and offline) is to get journalists and editors to approach you, as opposed to the other way around. To do this you need to become a valued source of information for the media. Here are some ways to turn your one-way relationship with the media (you send, they receive), into a two-way process (they ask, you give):

- Only send e-media releases when you have something of real media interest to shout about.
- Send releases at convenient times for journalists. This means well before deadlines and avoiding Mondays and Fridays.
- Contribute useful articles.
- Turn your site into a media source. Put press release archives on your site, with a keyword search facility.
- Be willing to provide information about your industry or profession as well as your business.

As well as following the above advice, you could also pay to be included on one of the online media resource sites such as the Experts Directory (www.experts.com) and GuestFinder (www.guestfinder.com). Journalists turn to these sites when they are researching a story and looking for a relevant expert to turn to for his or her authoritative opinion. Entrants are listed under categories relevant to their business area, and are given their own Web page that enables them to show off their specific credentials.

Summary

Building and sustaining your profile in the e-media is a suitable way of reaching your online audiences. People reading about your Web site in an e-zine or news site can then be browsing your site within a few clicks of their mouse.

Furthermore, generating media attention **online** can give a positive effect **offline**, as the next chapter will go on to explain.

fourteen

Crisis **e-PR**

For every journalist who is looking on the Internet for a positive business story, there are at least ten looking to dish the dirt on the latest online business disaster. Bad news makes the front page, while good news is relegated to page seventeen of the Sunday supplement; it's as simple as that. As Lord Northcliffe, the founder of the *Daily Mail*, once said: 'News is what somebody somewhere wants to suppress; all the rest is advertising'. With this in mind, the Internet affords great opportunities for the investigative journalist. By eavesdropping in newsgroups and mailing list discussion groups, the Net-savvy journalist can find all sorts of dirty laundry to give a good airing in the media. However, what represents an opportunity to the journalist constitutes a threat to the business. Intel, McDonalds, Shell, Apple, Netscape and, most frequently, Microsoft, have suffered as a result of letting negative issues develop online until the offline media pick them up and transform them into a crisis. It is not just the big guns either, who can fall foul of online controversy. Many small and medium-sized businesses have had their reputation tarnished online. Way back in 1996, for instance, a rumour about a now out-of-business cookie firm escalated online. The rumour, initiated by a competitor, stated that the firm had supplied their products to O J Simpson's victory party when he was acquitted of murder. Whether they did or not is uncertain. What is certain, however, is that the firm's reputation was tarnished so much in online newsgroups that the controversy spread offline, which proved fatal for the firm's already much tarnished reputation.

However, there is some good news. While the Internet may give people who have a grudge against your firm an attentive audience of similarly aggrieved individuals, it also gives businesses the opportunity to respond quickly and effectively to the spread of misinformation. The fact is that, online or offline, most crises can be predicted and therefore prevented.

They build up slowly over time and, in all but the rarest cases, it is only poor management that transforms an 'issue' into a 'crisis'. Although cyberspace gives your e-critics a voice they may not have elsewhere, it also allows you to predict, locate and respond to negative publicity with ease and efficiency. Nowhere else is the Internet's ability to make or break reputations better illustrated than in the area of crisis e-PR.

This chapter looks at the e-PR tools and strategies you will need to limit and manage negative publicity about your company online and keep your cyber reputation intact.

Newsgroup controversy and how to deal with it

Monitoring newsgroups is perhaps the most vital part of your e-PR crisis strategy. People with a complaint about your company can use these groups to express their dissatisfaction in front of an audience of thousands. People no longer need to go via a media gatekeeper, such as a journalist, as they have direct access to a mass readership themselves.

Consumers use online newsgroups to find information about products or services they may want to spend money on. If misinformation and blatant lies about your company are given an airing in one of these groups, they need to be checked as soon as possible. If they are not they will be read and quoted as fact.

Deja News

You do not need to spend hours each week searching the newsgroups for negative material about your business, as there are free services which will do it for you.

Use Deja News (http://www.dejanews.com) to find negative comments about your company.

Type in your keywords and Deja will respond with:

- the e-mail address of the person who wrote the article;
- the newsgroup(s) in which it was posted;

- the title of the message;
- additional information (previous messages, etc.) linked to the e-mail address and headline.

When you find negative comments about your business you will need to act, but what is the best way to respond? Here are some guidelines to follow when handling your e-critics:

- Respond quickly. The sooner misinformation is corrected the better. On the Internet, nothing travels faster than bad news.
- Be polite. Whatever tone the message you are responding to was written in, remain polite at all times as your message will be read by a lot of people.
- Avoid business or legal jargon.
- Reveal identities. If you or your employees are correcting misinformation, do not pretend to be another customer. Remember, every message can be traced.
- Find allies. Rally any loyal customers who contribute to the newsgroup and ask them to respond to other people's complaints.
- Get to know the moderators. The moderators of newsgroups can be very useful to you at a time of crisis. Correspond with them via e-mail on a regular basis, and provide them with suitable topics for discussion. If you look like you could be a useful member of the group, they may be willing to come to your rescue when controversy develops online.
- Admit problems. When a customer is right, acknowledge the fact and attempt to resolve it.
- Keep in correspondence with anyone who has made a complaint. If he or she has complained once, they are likely to do it again. Keep in contact so they feel they can talk to you, as opposed to an entire newsgroup, about any problem.
- Ask for feedback. The obvious way to avoid unwelcome criticism is to welcome it. By asking for customer opinion, you are more likely to get more constructive responses.
- Keep newsgroups informed. If problems occur, provide as much information as possible on how they can resolve them.

A note on netiquette: Although advertising and blatant commercialism are often frowned upon in newsgroups, no one objects to companies that simply want to set the record straight.

Media relations

It is not only your customers who participate in or read newsgroups. Journalists from newspapers and trade publications read newsgroups to gauge public opinion on products and services. One of your e-PR objectives should be to make sure journalists trust you as a valuable source of (reasonably) objective information about your company, so that they will turn to you before putting a negative story into print. After all, journalists will always find an angry customer willing to talk if you aren't ready and willing to provide the information they want for their article.

There are a number of ways the Internet can help build relations with reporters before, during and after difficult situations. Here are some tried and tested ways to help you limit negative media coverage.

Develop a media mailing list

Create a mailing list of key journalists who are likely to write about your business. Every time you see a relevant reporter's e-mail address, store it in an e-mail folder marked 'media mailing list'. This way, if a crisis occurs you can make immediate and simultaneous contact with every appropriate journalist. No journalist will therefore be able to complain that he or she has received information later than anyone else.

Use Bcc:

Remember: List the journalists' addresses in the Bcc: (blind carbon copy) box so they cannot see how many addresses you have sent it to. A journalist with a deflated ego will do little to help your crisis management programme.

Keep the list updated. Journalists (especially those online) can move to different publications or positions quite regularly. Keep track of changes and record them.

Hold an online press conference

If a crisis does break out you may consider holding an online media event to supplement or substitute a real world press conference. The advantages of conducting this type of event over the Internet include:

- Unlimited attendance. The freedom of cyberspace allows as many people to contribute to a conference as want to.
- No need for note taking. Everyone who attends can print a transcript of the entire event.
- Variety of audiences. Customers and investors as well as journalists can take part.

To hold an online press conference you need to set up a chat system (which can be done in a number of ways). One model is a special Java applet that you can download and run within the Web browser to manage and moderate online conferences. Another way is to install special software which allows you to run chat and conference sessions. Both ways allow you to set up areas that enable users to talk about a certain issue.

Once the chat system is up and running and you have mailing lists for each target audience you can send an e-mail at any time to your target audience specifying the time, date and topic of the conference.

Conference and chat systems:

- e-ware: http://www.eware.com
- i-chat: http://www.ichat.com
- Proxicom: http://www.proxicom.com

Set up an online media centre

To make sure journalists never feel the need to 'fill the gaps', it is a good idea to have as much information as possible about your company available at their fingertips. The easiest way to do this is to set up a media centre on your Web site that acts as a useful resource for journalists.

Key sections to include in an online media centre:

- latest company news;
- a press release archive (sort headlines by date and topic with links to the full text);
- annual reports;
- product/service information;
- financial reports;
- a press file of media extracts about your company;
- consumer opinion (positive and not-so-positive quotes from your customers);
- contact information;
- biographies of key members of the management team.

Distribute press releases online

Distributing press releases via e-mail has the obvious advantage of speed over using the postal service. Time is of the essence when a crisis arrives or is anticipated and e-mail allows you to get your message out in as much time as it takes you to think of it and type it out.

First, send out a press release to all the addresses on your media mailing list, then to one of the catch-all online news distribution services such as PR Newswire (http://www.prnewswire.com) or PR Web (http://www.prweb.com).

Provide media training

Every member of your company should be briefed on how to handle the media in the event of a crisis. The Internet's interactive nature makes it a good medium for training-session material. It can be used to train individuals separately or in a group.

- Use a chat facility such as iChat (http://www.ichat.com) to conduct crisis strategy meetings online.
- Send e-mails to all members of staff detailing how they should act when approached by the media in a crisis.

Anti-sites and how to handle them

Whereas most of this chapter deals with aspects of online crisis PR that mirror PR techniques in the real world (such as holding an online press conference), there is one feature of crisis e-PR that is unique to the Internet. This surrounds the question of 'anti-sites' that are set up to deliberately harm your company or business sector.

Whereas a couple of years ago the issue of 'anti-sites' only really affected major corporations such as Microsoft (http://www.microsucks.com) and Pizza Hut (http://www.pissahut.com), the rapid growth in popularity of these sites means any company, large or small, is a potential target. 'Anti-sites' serve to stir-up negative opinion by building an online community of similarly disgruntled individuals and placing it on a cyber soap box.

The worrying fact is that many companies are not even aware that they are being slurred online. Although the milder anti-sites can provide valuable company feedback, you should be keen to avoid having your business humiliated online.

But first you need to be aware of the different types of anti-sites out there:

- **Spoof sites.** Spoof sites are sites that look and feel like the company site they are mocking. U.S. West fell victim to a spoof site when one unhappy Net-literate customer decided to set up a 'U.S. Worst' site.
- **Hate sites.** Microsoft and McDonalds are probably the two most famous victims of hate sites. These sites do not aim for subtle parody or objectivity; their one and only aim is to cause as much damage as possible to your company. Hate sites are often set up by interest or pressure groups.
- **Opinion sites.** Opinion sites are generally set up by consumers who have a strong opinion about your company. These provide customers with another way of airing their feelings on the products and services you or your competitors provide. These can also provide journalists with newsworthy quotes for an article on your company.

Although these sites are difficult to put a stop to entirely, there are actions you can take to prevent anti-sites in the first place and, if they do occur, to turn a negative situation into positive PR:

- Register your company name as the domain name as soon as you decide to have a Web site.
- Set up, or motivate someone else to set up a non-official, pro-company site so that information can be presented in a more objective way. Sites that provide the middle ground between company and consumer can be the most effective e-PR sites of all.
- Monitor the issues raised in anti-sites and respond directly by private e-mail to customer complaints.
- Look out for anti-sites by conducting a search on Yahoo! using the keywords 'consumer opinions' along with the name of your company.

Case study: Intel and the professor

In 1997, a professor of mathematics found a glitch in Intel's Pentium chip. He discovered that the mathematical functions for the chip's complicated formula were not consistently accurate. The professor decided to send an article about his findings to a small academic newsgroup. Word spread through the university community and the editor of a trade title caught hold of the story. The general press then reported the professor's findings and sought Intel's response. Intel denied any major problem, declaring it would only affect a 'tiny percentage' of customers. They failed to take responsibility or replace the affected chips.

The issue grew online, as it became a key topic in an increasing number of online discussion groups, which kept on feeding the offline media. The share value dropped by over 20 points. It was only when IBM's declaration that they would not use Intel chips in their computers made the front page of the New York Times that Intel went back on their previous position and agreed to replace the chips. Even today, evidence can be found of how Intel's poor response to online criticism has affected its reputation on the Net. The 'Intel Secrets' site at http://www.x86.org/, which was set up at the time of the media's damning coverage of Intel's unhealthy chip, still emphasizes the faults to be found in various Intel products.

Anti-site case study: 'Dos and Donuts'

In 1999 Dunkin Donuts' parent company, Allied Domecq, started to grow concerned about a consumer opinion Web site located at http://www.dunkindonuts.org, when they realized it came above the official dot com site on most of the major search engines.

Rather than ignore the site in the vain hope it would eventually disappear, Allied Domecq and Dunkin Donuts monitored the 'anti-site' and frequently responded directly to complaints by private e-mail. Unhappy customers were offered vouchers and discounts and even one-to-one meetings with local store managers.

The site that was originally set up by disgruntled customer, David Felton, to vent anger at Dunkin Donuts' poor customer service, soon became a valuable resource for the company. Allied Domecq eventually managed to buy the site from Felton to turn it into an official customer feedback service. Felton later claimed the reason he was willing to sell the site was Dunkin Donuts' positive response to customer complaints and comments. Today, the site is still up and running and providing both company and consumer with a valuable and informative resource.

Summary

Misinformation about your company or Web site found in news-groups or on other Web sites will be considered as fact if left without monitoring. Online you must interact with employees, customers and journalists in a variety of ways if you are to predict and prevent crises. Your customers *will* talk to one another online so ignoring e-PR is no longer a valid option.

fifteen

E-PR **in the 'real world'**

Your e-PR activity should not exist in a vacuum. To make sure your messages are heard online, you need to provide effective support offline.

This chapter looks at the relationship between e-PR and the offline media, ways you can use the offline media to draw attention to your e-activity as well as ways of generating publicity beyond the media altogether. We will start by looking at the traditional media's fixation with the Internet.

A hot media topic

The Internet in general and the World Wide Web in particular are most definitely hot topics for the traditional media. Consider the immense media interest, on both sides of the Atlantic, in the effect dot com companies are having on the stock market.

From the financial pages of the broadsheets right through to the feature pages of consumer magazines, the Internet generates a phenomenal interest. Even if you believed that online audiences were irrelevant to your business (although, I have to say, you look far too intelligent to think that), a strong Web presence could still be used as a PR hook for the offline media.

When Pizza Hut announced you could order pizzas online, the media coverage offline reached far more people than they could via the Internet alone. This is one of many instances where the Internet causes bigger waves offline than it could ever do online.

Finding the right angle

Although the Internet is still a very media-friendly topic, its novelty value is beginning to wane. As mentioned above, simply having a Web site is no longer a guarantee of media interest, as every business is now expected to have a presence on the Web. The offline media are after Internet stories with the right hook.

Pizza Hut managed to provide the right hook with their 'Order Pizzas Online' story for the following reasons:

- It demonstrated how the Internet can relate to the real world.
- Pizza Hut provided journalists with something of novelty value (they were the *first* company to offer this service online). This was definitely a 'man bites dog story'.
- The story centred on the effect this would have on the consumer at large.
- Pizza Hut is a recognized brand of international interest. To find the perfect angle you need to think of a novel way your Web site can reach beyond cyberspace into the real world (see Figure 15.1).

Even if your business is not widely known, you can make your Internet-based story of general interest by associating it with something or someone of broader concern. Two of the main ways you can do this are through endorsement and sponsorship.

Endorsement

Third-party endorsement, which has been discussed elsewhere in this book, is an especially effective way of attracting the attention of the offline media.

Ask relevant well-known people outside your company (academics, celebrities, entrepreneurs, politicians, industry figures, etc) to get involved with your site. Think of the benefits they could get out of such an endorsement and put a proposal together. They may be more likely to promote your site if you provide them with an opportunity to plug their own projects from your site.

If you have relevant personal contacts who would be willing to add weight to your site's media profile, so much the better.

Figure 15.1 The Pizza Hut home page

Sponsorship

If you find a relevant opportunity, sponsorship can be an ideal way of generating publicity for your Web site.

Online and offline sponsorship can enhance your reputation within traditional media through associating your name with something of a broader interest.

The way sponsorship works is simple: you contribute funds towards an event, Web site, charity, team or whatever in return for promotional opportunities of various sorts.

The benefits of sponsorship include:

- An increase in awareness of your Web site.
- Another hook to get the offline media interested in your site.
- The ability to improve the image of your business. This is particularly the case if you choose to sponsor a charity, free information Web site or other not-for-profit organization.
- It offers an active way of targeting individual publics. If a significant percentage of your target audience is interested in the

Arts, you could sponsor an art exhibition and make people associate your Web site with their interest in Picasso.

■ Sponsorship can strengthen brand identity by accentuating key attributes. Sponsoring the Picasso exhibition, for instance, could help consolidate the sense of good taste and culture you seek to associate with your Web site.

Sponsorship is an effective way of getting your site noticed beyond cyberspace, and is accessible to most businesses. If you have a relatively small e-PR budget for your food and drink Web site, for instance, sponsoring a restaurant (or small chain of restaurants) and placing your URL (Web site address) at the foot of the menu could prove a tasty option.

Relating to the real world

Whereas what used to fascinate journalists was how alien and unrelated the Internet was to the world of 'bricks and mortar', now the opposite holds true.

People now understand that the Internet **will** change their lives; they just want to know exactly **how** it will do this. The media appreciate this and therefore want to get hold of as many stories as possible, which throw light on the relationship between cyberspace and the real world.

The most media-friendly online companies, such as Amazon.com, LastMinute.com and Let's Buy It.com, can easily capture the public's imagination by relating to the real world (see Figure 15.2). Keeping this in mind, here are some ways to make your Web site relevant to the interests of the traditional media:

■ Simulate aspects of the real world on your site. Amazon has caught the public's imagination to such an extent because it has taken something as traditional and tangible as a high-street bookstore and transferred it to cyberspace.

■ Deliver your products to the homes of your customers. E-commerce sites tend to have the media advantage over other forms of Web sites as they can, quite literally, use the Internet to cause a real-world action (the delivery of a product to the consumer's door).

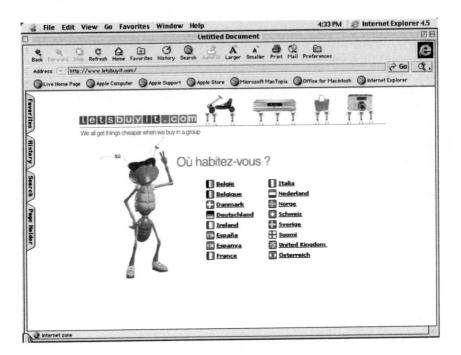

Figure 15.2 Lets Buy It.com replicates aspects of real world shopping onto its site

■ Think in terms of online cause and offline effect. By constantly thinking of the effect your site has on its audience in the physical world you will be viewing it from the perspective of the offline media.

Sending e-media releases to the offline media

The previous chapter details how you should put an e-media release together for the online media. The same form can be applied when targeting the traditional print and broadcast media. The only thing you should do differently is sending a print version of the release by fax or post along with the online version.

E-mail addresses and other media contact details for the offline media can be found at Media UK (http://www.mediauk.com) and the other media directories referred to in the last chapter. Trawl through the radio, TV, magazine, newspaper and trade publications and compile a list of relevant offline media contacts.

Contrary to the situation with online media, in the traditional media deadlines are everything. For a release to have maximum impact it needs to be timed right. This means finding out publications and deadline dates. Releases need to be sent well in advance of a deadline for them to be given the editorial go-ahead.

If you decide to post as well as e-mail your releases make sure you post your release a day in advance of your e-mail to ensure that both arrive on the same day.

If your release has a general cross-media appeal, it may be worthwhile to use one of the new breed of online PR services which can distribute releases on your behalf. This means your release can be sent to journalists and editors you don't even know about. Among the services that offer the biggest and broadest sweep there are PR Newswire, Business Wire, PR Web and Press Wire.

PR Newswire (http://www.prnewswire.com)

PR Newswire is one of the largest release distribution services on the Web (see Figure 15.3). Providing distribution services worldwide, PR newswire offers a customized service for businesses seeking as wide a reach as possible. It can also target the media down to specific categories and offers various fax, as well as online, services.

Fees are worked out on a number of words basis, as well as on how many journalists will receive the release. As a result, charges vary widely.

As PR Newswire is respected by journalists and PR people alike, your release is likely to be included on other online resources. For instance, Excite (http://www.excite.com) picks up releases for PR newswire and puts them on their News Tracker pages. The positive knock-on effect of using this service can therefore be immense.

Business Wire (http://www.businesswire.com)

Business Wire also distributes releases around the globe, to TV, radio, print, wire services and other media. Although it charges a US $100 (or equivalent) membership fee, its distribution system is

Figure 15.3 PR Newswire offers a tailor-made distribution service for media releases

more sophisticated. It can distribute to individual geographical regions and special interest markets (arts media, IT Media, student publications, etc) as well as offering a media monitoring service.

PR Web (http://www.prWeb.com)

PR Web is an increasingly popular free distribution service. Although its database is not quite as vast as PR Newswire or Business Wire, it can target distribution to specific media sectors. It also provides one of the more user-friendly services. Once you have your release ready for distribution, go to the site, fill in a brief form and the release is automatically sent out.

Presswire (http://www.presswire.com)

Presswire offers both paid-for and free services.

Supplementing e-PR with offline methods

There are many instances when offline activities become part of an e-PR strategy. Here are some offline communication tools that can help you meet your e-PR objectives.

The phone

As e-mail and telecommunications technology (especially WAP) moves ever closer together, e-mail messages are increasingly being combined with an accompanying phone call and vice versa.

The ways you can use the phone to supplement your e-PR efforts include:

- **Follow-up calls.** After e-mailing press releases or other important messages, a follow-up call can make a big difference and gives you the chance to clear up any points that may have caused confusion.
- **Contact numbers.** A contact telephone number is essential somewhere on your Web site, at the foot of your press releases and in your online newsletters. It can also be included in your e-mail signature line.
- **Hotlines.** In the event of a crisis or when you expect a surge of consumer interest, you should set up a Freephone hotline to prevent an overload of e-mails.
- **Networking.** The phone is a great networking aid, allowing you to communicate on a personal level to journalists and consumers.

The post

Derogatively termed 'snail mail' by committed Net heads, the postal service does seem a little expensive and time consuming when compared with the efficiency of e-mail.

It can, however, be used to limit the e-mail overload journalists can often be heard to complain about. You can also mail printed newsletters and brochures promoting your Web site to create interest in your online activity. When you need to be sure that a message gets through to someone, you should not rely on e-mail alone. The phenomenal amount of 'spam' (unwanted and unsolicited e-mail) some people receive has led to a certain cynicism over any e-mail message from an unfamiliar address. As a result, many people have set up filtering systems that eliminate certain types of e-mail before they are read. Even if they haven't, some people are so over burdened with e-mail messages they don't bother reading any of them. The postal service therefore provides a worthy (albeit more expensive) alternative and supplement for when you need to combat e-mail fatigue.

The fax

As the Internet revolution races on, the humble fax machine is starting to look a little out of breath. However, there are times when the fax provides valuable e-PR support. For instance, faxing and e-mailing a press release simultaneously lend your story a greater sense of urgency than it would have if you were to send the release via post. Your fax number should be included alongside your phone number wherever it appears online.

Internet magazines

The fact that the offline media are fascinated and fixated by the Internet is evidenced by the explosion of print magazines covering the topic. These publications are the ideal place for you to promote your online activity, as their readers have an active interest in all things Internet. There are two main ways to gain coverage in these publications:

- Send press releases about your Web site to relevant journalists. Many magazines include a 'Sites of the Month' feature; make sure the people who compile this section are made aware of your site through regular press releases.
- Write an article. One way to boost your status as an Internet authority is to write an article on an area relevant to your Internet experience. Editors are always looking to add to their list of freelancers providing your ideas are appropriate for their publication. If you have an idea of whom the magazine appeals to, writing a relevant article should not be too difficult. Contact

the editor via e-mail in the first instance with a proposal (as opposed to a full article). Then follow up with a telephone call the next day.

'Advertorials'

Between PR and advertising, you have the 'advertorial' or paid editorial. The advantage of 'advertorials' is that you have complete control over what is written; the disadvantage is that you have to pay for the privilege.

Both online and offline, the use of 'advertorials' is on the increase, as benefits can be great for the advertiser and the publication alike.

You can use offline 'advertorials' to tell a specific audience about your online presence, as they can be very effective means of getting the word out.

Advertising

Advertising is the friend, not foe, of PR and can be used to bolster your online and offline PR efforts.

Other print media

As well as Internet magazines, other consumer magazines and newspapers are devoting an increasing amount of column inches to the Internet.

You should identify the journalists most likely to write about your Web site, and keep him or her informed about any changes or additions to your site or about any other aspect of your e-PR activity of general interest.

Other print publications you should target include:

- trade publications relevant to your business sector;
- consumer magazines appealing to your target audience;
- business directories;
- newsletters and other house publications issued by trade associations and other appropriate organizations.

Again, as well as sending press releases about your Web site you should submit ideas to the relevant editor and offer to write articles.

If you are not confident in your skills as a writer, find a colleague who can.

TV

The medium with the closest affiliation with the Internet is television. It will not be long before the Internet will be accessible through TV sets and when this happens the integration of both media will be complete. Already there is a strong overlap. The Internet is beginning to resemble TV with online audiovisual technology improving quickly and with the increasing popularity of the Web-cam. Furthermore, TV programmes are increasingly asking for viewers to e-mail contributions that are broadcast before the end of a show.

There are even TV series completely devoted to the Internet (such as Channel Four's *Dot Comedy*).

Most major TV stations have a strong Web presence (CNN and the BBC clearly both take the Internet *very* seriously), and receive a lot of financial support (in terms of advertising revenue) from the prolific dot com companies.

Despite the close partnership of both media, TV remains the most difficult place to gain publicity for your online venture. TV stations take a very cynical view of any business, online or offline, seeking 'free' advertising space. In contrast, much of the news non-commercial organizations are disseminating is greeted with open arms by TV news and feature editors. However, you can use this situation to your advantage in the following ways:

- Sponsor a non-commercial event. TV stations will often want to publicize a charitable event, even if your business is also likely to benefit. Sports and arts events provide similar opportunities.
- Take issue with a trade association. Trade associations and professional bodies are more likely to gain TV coverage than individual companies because they represent interests across an industry. By taking issue with, or supporting, any actions or decisions they make, you can often gain TV coverage yourself.
- Target Internet-based TV programmes. Where you do want to gain publicity for yourself independent of other organizations, your best bet is to target the new breed of programmes that focus entirely on Internet issues.

Radio

The first electronic medium and the original form of cyberspace, radio, can be a very effective means of promoting your Web site. The growing number of national and regional stations, combined with the ever-growing popularity of 'talk radio', means there are limitless possibilities for you to promote your Internet activities.

Like TV, radio is merging with the Internet in a number of ways and often radio stations are broadcast on air and online at the same time. Here are some possibilities for you to think about:

- **Phone-ins.** Radio phone-ins can be used in one of two ways. You can either contribute to the show as a caller or, preferably, appear on a phone-in show as an expert. To pursue the second option, simply identify relevant programmes, then contact the producer or editor at the show telling him or her why you (or a colleague) would be a good guest for the show.
- **Chat rooms.** Many radio shows with their own Web sites have online chat rooms. After a show, a special guest may be invited to field questions on a certain topic. This provides a fantastic way of combining the power of radio and the Internet to show off your expertise and even lead people to your site.
- **Competitions.** Both music and talk-based radio shows love to hold competitions. Get involved by offering your products or services as a prize, and get a plug for your Web site in return.

Beyond the media

There are many ways to support your e-PR efforts without the help of editors and journalists. Here are some of them:

- **Take part in exhibitions.** The Internet can be used as a hook to involve people at your stand in a trade fair or exhibition. You can take people on a tour of your site, get them to subscribe to your online newsletter or hand out CD ROMs with your Web site and other online material. You could participate in the rising number of Internet exhibitions as well as those that relate more specifically to your business area. Furthermore, you can use the Internet as a means of researching which exhibitions would be right for your business. I have found the search engines AltaVista (http://www.altavista.com) and Lycos (http://www.lycos.com) particularly useful ways of finding out about relevant exhibitions. Simply type in the keywords 'exhibitions + Internet' or similar combinations relating to your business.

- **Hold a party.** Holding a party is one way to mark momentous occasions in the life of your Web site (its launch, birthday, makeover and so on). This technique can prove particularly useful in winning over key audiences such as journalists or stakeholders.
- **Brand your stationery.** Your e-mail and Web site addresses should appear prominently on your brochures, letterheads, business cards and any other printed stationery you may have. To highlight the importance of your Web site you could print stickers with nothing on except your URL and use them as a seal on your envelopes.
- **Generate word of mouth publicity.** Tell everyone you meet how excited you are about your Web site and your other online activity. Encourage your colleagues to do the same.
- **Send mail shots.** You can send out letters, brochures and even CD ROMs to promote your site. Make sure your letters are as targeted and personal as possible (find out the name of the right person to send your mailing to in advance).

Summary

Until we are at the stage when the Internet has fully merged with other media, e-PR needs to be supplemented and supported by offline PR activity. After all, people who log on to the Internet are the same people who read magazines, watch TV, listen to the radio, receive mail and go out to parties. Although it can often be easy to forget, people **live** in the real world, they only *visit* cyberspace. As communication tools are becoming more integrated, e-PR is moving into the 'real world' of TV sets and mobile phones. This could lead to more e-PR power for your business by creating more effective communications combining the strengths of the existing media.

sixteen

Glossary

address book An online directory in a Web browser where you can store and manage e-mail addresses.

article The name given to a single contribution posted to a newsgroup.

associate programme A mutually beneficial partnership between sites.

attachment A file added to an e-mail to be sent via the e-mail system.

audience Refers to each individual section of your online public. Each business has various audiences (customers, investors, journalists, etc).

banner ad An online advertisement in the form of a band of text and graphics. Banner ads generally contain a hypertext link to the advertiser's site.

binaries Files attached to newsgroup articles, usually in the form of images of zip files.

bookmark A software tool that automatically loads the page it refers to.

browser Software that allows you to access the Internet and World Wide Web. Internet Explorer and Netscape Navigator are the most commonly used browsers.

bulletin board Software that provides an e-mail database where people can access and leave messages.

cancel option Useful in mail and newsgroup systems; allows you to delete a message before or just after posting an e-mail message or newsgroup article.

chat system   Enables users to have an interactive, typed conversation. Chat systems therefore build an online network of people who interact not just with the Web page but with other users as well.

click through   This refers to the act of clicking on a link to be transported to another site. The phrase is most commonly used in the context of banner advertising.

community   A group of Internet users with a shared interest or concept who interact with one another in newsgroups, mailing list discussion groups and other online interactive forums.

content services   Sites dedicated to a particular topic.

crawler   A type of search engine 'robot'.

cross-posting   The act of posting the same messages into several different news or discussion groups simultaneously.

cyberspace   Term originally coined in the sci-fi novels of William Burroughs, referring to the online world and its communication networks and evoking its intangible sense of space.

distribution list   A list of e-mail addresses given one collective title. You can send a message to all the addresses simultaneously by referring to the list title.

domain name   A domain name consists of two components: a first-level domain (identifying the organization or computer hosting a Web site) and a second-level domain (-.com, -.org, -.co.uk, etc). A domain name not only forms part of Web site addresses but is also used after the '@' in e-mail.

download   The term used to describe the transfer of a computer file from a server to a PC, Mac or other computer technology.

e-business   The catch-all term referring to the business world online. It also signifies an individual online business or company.

e-commerce   A generic term used to refer to everything that surrounds business transactions over the Internet.

e-journalists   Journalists and editors working for the e-media.

e-mail   Electronic mail. A message sent across the Internet, or the act of transferring messages between computers, mobile phones or other communications attached to the Internet.

e-mail system   The collective e-mail software systems that allow you to create, send and receive e-mail messages.

e-media   Online media. In the context of e-PR the term specifically refers to 'third-party e-media' or e-media beyond your immediate control.

e-media relations   The practice of building relations with editors and journalists via the Internet, especially when they work for the e-media.

e-media release   An online, interactive press release sent via the e-mail system.

e-PR   Electronic public relations. The practice of managing reputations and building relevant relationships online. Every aspect of e-business activity can be seen from an e-PR perspective.

e-zines   Online interactive magazines.

emoticons   Common symbols used in e-mail and newsgroup messages to denote particular emotions by resembling faces on their side. :-) therefore indicates happiness (a smiley face), while :-(conveys unhappiness (an unhappy face). The word 'emoticon' is a hybrid of 'emotion' and 'icon'. 'Emoticons' are generally deemed bad e-PR practice and are inappropriate for business communications.

filter   Software that can discriminate between types of incoming and ongoing e-mail messages.

flame   A 'heated' and hostile message posted in a newsgroup, usually in response to **spam**; also, the act of posting such a message.

form   A means of collecting data on Web pages, using text boxes, radio buttons and other facilities. Forms are used as a way of making sites more interactive as well as for sales and marketing purposes.

forums   Newsgroups, mailing list discussion groups, chat rooms and other online areas that allow you to read, post and respond to messages.

freebies   Free products given away as incentives to attract Web site visitors.

freeware   Free software programs.

GIF   Short for graphic information file. Used on the Internet to display files that contain graphic images.

groupware   A set of technology tools enabling businesses to share software.

history list   A record of visited Web pages you can access through your browser. It can help you find sites you haven't been able to bookmark.

hit counters   Software that records hits as opposed to unique impressions.

hits   A hit is a transfer from a server to a browser. Each time a browser transfers a text page that has no graphics it represents one hit. If the page has a graphic inside it, those are two hits. If it has two graphics, those are three hits and so on. Hits therefore do not provide an accurate measurement of the number of times your Web site has been visited.

home page   The first and/or main page on a Web site.

host computer   A computer connected to the Internet.

HTML   Hypertext Mark-up Language. A computer code used to build and develop Web pages.

hyper time   Internet time. Referring to the fact that Internet time moves faster than real-world time.

hypertext links   Generally found on Web pages (although they can be used in e-mail messages), hypertext links link onto HTML pages and documents.

information overload   The situation of having so much information on your site as to bore or intimidate your customer.

Internet   The global network of computers accessed with the aid of a modem. The Internet includes Web sites, e-mail, newsgroups and other forums. This is a public network, though many of the computers connected to it are also part of **Intranets**.

Intranet   Internal, private computer networks using Internet technology to facilitate communication between individuals within organizations.

IRC   Internet Relay Chat (see **chat**).

ISP   Internet Service Provider. A firm that provides Internet services such as e-mail and Web hosting facilities.

itchy finger syndrome   A slang reference to the Internet user's hunger for interactivity.

junk mail   See **spam**.

keywords   Words used by search engines to help find and register sites.

kill file   An instruction used in a newsgroup by your newsreader to skip particular articles, according to criteria you specify.

links   Text or graphic icons that move you to different Web pages or sites. Links are activated by clicking them with a mouse.

list server   Mailing list software.

log on/off   To access/leave the Internet.

lurk   To read messages in newsgroups or mailing list discussion groups, but not post anything yourself.

mail server   A remote computer (usually your ISP) enabling you to send and receive messages via e-mail software.

mailing list   A collection of e-mail addresses.

meta tags   The keyword and description commands used in your Web page code used to help search engines index your Web site.

modem   Modulator/demodulator. This is an internal or external piece of hardware that works with your PC or Mac. It links into a phone socket enabling computer-based information to be transmitted over a phone network.

moderator   Someone in charge of a newsgroup, mailing list discussion group or similar forum. The moderator censors any unwelcome articles.

multi-phased medium   A medium, such as the Internet, which uses a variety of means for a variety of ends.

navigation   The way a visitor travels around, or is directed around a Web site, via links.

net   Shorthand for Internet.

net head   Internet obsessed individual.

netiquette   The etiquette of the Internet. It is used mainly in the context of e-mail and newsgroup communication.

newbie   Slang term for a new newsgroup member.

newsgroups   Collectively referred to as the 'Usenet', newsgroups are online discussion areas. People post messages to the groups that all the other members can read. There are over 50,000 active newsgroups on the Internet covering topics as diverse as Social Welfare Reform and South Park.

newsreader   Software enabling you to search, read, post and arrange newsgroup messages.

niche   A narrow but unified market or audience segment. The Internet is particularly suited to niche markets and audiences.

NNTP   Network News Transport Protocol. In newsgroups, NNTP is the method by which newsreader software communicates with news servers across the Internet.

offline   Used to denote any activity or situation that does not involve being connected to the Internet.

online   The state of being connected via a modem to the Internet.

operating system   Software stored in a computer that controls hardware components and the processes that run on them.

plain text   Text that is encoded and contains no layout information; non-HTML text.

post   The act of sending an article to a newsgroup.

rank   A search engine position.

real world   Everything outside the Internet.

refresh   The act of reloading a Web site or page.

robot   A tool used by search engines to find and examine Web sites.

search engine   A site that enables you to conduct a keyword search of indexed information on its database. Also refers to the software used in this process.

secure server   Hardware and software that secure e-commerce credit card transactions so there is no risk of people gaining access to credit card details online.

signature (file)   Information appended to the end of a message that identifies the sender's details.

smiley   See **emoticon**.

spam   Junk mail on the Internet, normally in the form of unsolicited and unwelcome e-mail messages. The term is used most frequently in the context of newsgroups referring to the same article being posted repeatedly to different newsgroups. The term is a reference to the famous Monty Python 'spam, spam, spam' sketch where 'spam' is served with everything.

snail mail   Net-head term for the 'real world' postal service.

snooze news   Company 'news' which will not interest journalists or editors.

spider   A type of search engine 'robot'.

sysop   Systems operator. See **moderator**.

system administrator   Someone responsible for the management of an e-mail system.

thread   An ongoing newsgroup topic.

traffic   The flow of unique visitors to your site.

trolling   The act of posting a newsgroup article with the deliberate intent of provoking a heated or **flamed** response.

URL   Uniform Resource Locator. A full Web address, for example: http//www.yac.com

Usenet   The system that distributes newsgroups; also the collective term for newsgroups.

visitors   The people who come to your Web site.

Webmaster   Someone in charge of a Web site.

Web page   A single document stored at a Web site. A single Web browser window displays a single Web page at a time.

Web rings   Collections or communities of different Web sites and pages.

Web site   A collection of Web pages accessed via one URL.

World Wide Web   The World Wide Web does not mean the Internet. The World Wide Web is, in fact, a software system running across the Internet. It consists of (literally) billions of Web pages, usually containing text, images and HTML links.

index

16.2